THE MACMILLAN BOOK OF
EARLIEST CHRISTIAN MEDITATIONS

THE

MACMILLAN BOOK OF

EARLIEST CHRISTIAN MEDITATIONS

EDITED BY

F. Forrester Church

AND

Terrence J. Mulry

Macmillan Publishing Company
NEW YORK
Collier Macmillan Publishers
LONDON

Copyright © 1989 by F. Forrester Church and Terrence J. Mulry

All rights reserved. No part of this book may be reproduced or
transmitted in any form or by any means, electronic or mechanical,
including photocopying, recording, or by any information storage and
retrieval system, without permission in writing from the Publisher.

Macmillan Publishing Company
866 Third Avenue, New York, NY 10022
Collier Macmillan Canada, Inc.

Library of Congress Cataloging-in-Publication Data
The Macmillan book of earliest Christian meditations/edited by F.
    Forrester Church and Terrence J. Mulry.
        p.   cm.
    Includes index.
    ISBN 0-02-525582-7
    1. Meditations—Early works to 600.   I. Church, F. Forrester.
II. Mulry, Terrence J.   III. Title: Earliest Christian meditations.
BV4801.M33   1989
242'.09'015—dc 19   88-38487   CIP

Macmillan books are available at special discounts for bulk purchases for
sales promotions, premiums, fund-raising, or educational use. For details,
contact:

    Special Sales Director
    Macmillan Publishing Company
    866 Third Avenue
    New York, NY 10022

10 9 8 7 6 5 4 3 2 1

Printed in the United States of America

015
Flagstaff Public Library
Flagstaff, Arizona

242.09015
M107

CONTENTS

VII. MYSTICAL WISDOM

PREFACE

MY dictionary defines the word meditation in three ways: (1) the act of meditating—serious and sustained reflection or mental contemplation; (2) in religious use, the continuous application of the mind to the contemplation of some religious truth, mystery, or object of reverence as a devotional exercise; and (3) a discourse written or spoken of a meditative character. Accordingly, meditation is both a process (the act of meditating) and that upon which one meditates (writings of a contemplative character). In *The Macmillan Book of Earliest Christian Meditations* both senses of the word come into play. Drawing from the rich devotional literature of the first six centuries of our common era, we have selected representative Christian meditations in the hope of facilitating your own meditational devotions.

This book is the third of a trilogy that also includes *The Macmillan Book of Earliest Christian Prayers* and *The Macmillan Book of Earliest Christian Hymns.* Our intention remains as stated in the first two volumes: not to produce a carefully annotated scholarly work but rather to offer an accessible ("user friendly") collection of devotional literature for the spiritual refreshment of lay people, ministers, and scholars.

Though we don't presume to have isolated a precise genre of devotional writing, as you reflect upon these meditations you will find, in all their variety, any number of silver threads connecting one to another. One distinctive quality uniting these pieces is that they ponder, and invite us to ponder, not so much the nature of good and evil but rather the nature of right and wrong, or as

Origen said, "the contemplation of vice and virtue." In almost every instance, theological reflection is elevated by ethical consequence. The central theme is not so much "the good life" as it is a life lived in faithfulness to God.

The first principle of every meditation is that it should instruct the reader by offering moral or spiritual edification to facilitate the development of understanding and conscience. In this respect, the earliest Christian meditations are related both to the Jewish wisdom literature and to certain modes of Greek and Latin moral philosophy. Pre-Christian Jewish examples include the Book of Proverbs and Ecclesiastes from the Hebrew scriptures and the Book of Ecclesiasticus from the Old Testament Apocrypha. Greek and Latin meditations range from the moral teachings of Epicurus to Cicero.

Both traditions continued to flourish during the early years of Christianity. The former is manifest in the Sayings of the Fathers (or *Pirke Aboth*) and the Jewish philosopher Philo's *The Contemplative Life,* which are his reflections on an early monastic community, the Therapeutae. The latter contains such important writings as Marcus Aurelius's *Meditations* and Seneca's dialogues. The earliest Christian meditations reflect and develop these two strands of literature. Many of them, in fact, are cast in forms long familiar to one tradition or the other—the instructional dialogue, or discourse; the ethical letter; the theological essay; the exegetical homily; and the sayings collection.

This anthology is divided into seven sections (each with a brief introduction) and includes thirteen chapters.

Section I: "The Source" is a single chapter devoted to "Selections from the New Testament." It features the sayings of Jesus as well as excerpts from two Epistles that may be considered meditations, Hebrews and James.

Section II: "The Blossoming of Reflection: Second-Century Meditations" includes a chapter devoted to the second-century fathers and a chapter of Gnostic writings from the Nag Hammadi library.

Section III: "Out of Africa: Third-Century Meditations" presents in two chapters the contrasting teachings of two distinct approaches to early Christianity—"The African Tradition," which contains the Latin writings of Tertullian, Cyprian, and Commodian, and "The Alexandrian School," which features Greek works by Clement and Origen.

Section IV: "Wisdom from the Desert" offers the meditations of early Christian monks—the Greek-speaking Evagrius Ponticus, the Latin-speaking John Cassian, and the Coptic Desert Fathers.

Section V: "Episcopal Wisdom: Fourth-Century Meditations" features the meditations of four bishops—Saint Ambrose's *Duties of the Clergy*, which has been likened to the meditations of Cicero and Marcus Aurelius, and selected writings from Saint Athanasius, Saint Gregory of Nazianzus, and Saint Gregory of Nyssa.

Section VI: "Two Pillars of the Church: Fifth-Century Meditations" focuses on the devotional writings of Saint Augustine and Saint John Chrysostom.

Section VII: "Mystical Wisdom" concludes our offering of earliest Christian meditations with a soaring devotional piece from the turn of the sixth century by Pseudo-Dionysius.

Almost all of the selections included here are in the public domain, but we do wish to acknowledge and thank those who have given us permission to republish translations which are not: *The Praktikos of Evagrius Ponticus*, translated and edited by John Eudes Bamberger (Kalamazoo, Mich.: Cistercian Publications, 1970); *The Nag Hammadi Library in English*, edited by James Robinson, et al. (New York: Harper & Row, 1977); and *The Desert Fathers,* translated by Helen Waddell (Ann Arbor, Mich.: University of Michigan, 1957).

This book is dedicated to our teacher, Helmut Koester, professor at Harvard Divinity School. Helmut guided me kindly and wisely through my doctoral studies and dissertation on the Coptic Gospel of Thomas. He has also been a mentor for my co-editor Terrence Mulry during Terry's years as a student in the master of divinity program at HDS. Among the many things he has taught us is how intricately connected the strands and genres of Greek, Roman, Jewish, and Christian literature are. Helmut's insights helped to bring early Christian literature alive for both of us. Our dedication to bringing it alive for others is one fruit of his gentle passion and loving instruction.

F. FORRESTER CHURCH

I. The Source

Whosoever heareth these sayings of mine, and doeth
them, I will liken him unto a wise man,
which built his house upon a rock.

MATTHEW 7:24

THE New Testament, especially in its presentation of Jesus' own sayings, is both the primary source and principle model for all the meditations to follow. Well before the New Testament assumed the form familiar to us today, Jesus' parables and other teachings were collected by his followers, committed to memory, and finally recorded in writing. There were several such collections. One was used in the preparation of Mark's Gospel. Another, the so-called Q collection (for *Quelle* or "source" in German), was, together with Mark, utilized by Matthew and Luke. The Nag Hammadi library, the collection of papyri unearthed in the sands of Egypt in 1945, contains another early "sayings" collection, *The Gospel of Thomas,* 113 sayings of Jesus, some unique to this gospel, and others variations on familiar texts.

This genre is not unique to early Christianity, for its roots are planted deep in Jewish wisdom literature. The most familiar examples are the Book of Proverbs from the Hebrew Scriptures and Ecclesiasticus (or the Wisdom of Ben Sirah) from the Old Testament Apocrypha. Sayings from a single teacher or school would be gathered like a string of pearls—each distinctive but all united by voice or theme. There is little or no narrative in such collections. Often a single saying will stand on its own as a subject for contemplation. In other instances, the editors of these collections place teachings on similar topics or themes next to one another, thus offering the reader a broader context for reflection. Later, as adapted in the Gospels, these sayings are given a specific frame of reference. For instance, in the Sermon on the Mount from Matthew, several of Jesus' principle teachings are woven into a single sermon. Another variation, popular in Jewish apocalypic literature and adapted in many ways throughout the first Christian centuries, is the revelatory discourse—sayings linked together in response to students' or disciples' questions (for example, Jesus'

farewell discourses in the Gospel of John). We also include a
selection of parables from the Gospel of Mark and the Gospel of
Luke. The parable is a form of teaching particularly favored by
Jesus and offers, in many ways, the quintessential New Testament
meditation.

A different model, the exegetical discourse, is represented by
selections from two Epistles, Hebrews and James. Both are extended meditations—one emphasizing the primacy of faith, the
other the saving importance of works. There are parallels in each to
Greek and Latin philosophical or moral epistles as well as to
instructional writings from the Jewish wisdom tradition.

These two genres—sayings collections and homiletic discourses—are in one way or another reflected (or refracted) in the
meditations to follow.

ONE

Selections from the New Testament

AND seeing the multitudes, he went up into a mountain, and when he was set, his disciples came unto him:

And he opened his mouth, and taught them, saying,

Blessed are the poor in spirit, for theirs is the kingdom of heaven.

Blessed are they that mourn, for they shall be comforted.

Blessed are the meek, for they shall inherit the earth.

Blessed are they which do hunger and thirst after righteousness, for they shall be filled.

Blessed are the merciful, for they shall obtain mercy.

Blessed are the pure in heart, for they shall see God.

Blessed are the peacemakers, for they shall be called the children of God.

Blessed are they which are persecuted for righteousness' sake, for theirs is the kingdom of Heaven.

MATTHEW 5:1–10

YE have heard that it was said by them of old time, Thou shalt not kill; and whosoever shall kill shall be in danger of the judgment:

But I say unto you, That whosoever is angry with his
brother without a cause shall be in danger of the judgment,
and whosoever shall say to his brother, Raca, shall be in
danger of the council; but whosoever shall say, Thou fool,
shall be in danger of hell fire.

Therefore if thou bring thy gift to the altar, and there
rememberest that thy brother hath ought against thee;

Leave there thy gift before the altar, and go thy way;
first be reconciled to thy brother, and then come and offer
thy gift.

MATTHEW 5:21–24

YE have heard that it hath been said, An eye for an eye,
and a tooth for a tooth:

But I say unto you, That ye resist not evil: but
whosoever shall smite thee on thy right cheek, turn to him
the other also.

And if any man will sue thee at the law, and take away
thy coat, let him have thy cloak also.

And whosoever shall compel thee to go a mile, go
with him twain.

Give to him that asketh thee, and from him that would
borrow of thee turn not thou away.

Ye have heard that it hath been said, Thou shalt love
thy neighbor, and hate thine enemy.

But I say unto you, Love your enemies, bless them
that curse you, do good to them that hate you, and pray
for them which despitefully use you, and persecute you;

That ye may be the children of your Father which is in
Heaven, for he maketh his sun to rise on the evil and on
the good, and sendeth rain on the just and on the unjust.

MATTHEW 5:38–45

LAY not up for yourselves treasures upon earth, where moth and rust doth corrupt, and where thieves break through and steal;

But lay up for yourselves treasures in Heaven, where neither moth nor rust doth corrupt, and where thieves do not break through nor steal;

For where your treasure is, there will your heart be also.

MATTHEW 6:19–21

JUDGE not, that ye be not judged.

For with what judgment ye judge, ye shall be judged: and with what measure ye mete, it shall be measured to you again.

And why beholdest thou the mote that is in thy brother's eye, but considerest not the beam that is in thine own eye?

Or how wilt thou say to thy brother, Let me pull out the mote out of thine eye; and, behold, a beam is in thine own eye?

Thou hypocrite, first cast out the beam out of thine own eye; and then shalt thou see clearly to cast out the mote out of thy brother's eye.

MATTHEW 7:1–5

BEWARE of false prophets, which come to you in sheep's clothing, but inwardly they are ravening wolves.

Ye shall know them by their fruits. Do men gather grapes of thorns, or figs of thistles?

Even so every good tree bringeth forth good fruit; but a corrupt tree bringeth forth evil fruit.

A good tree cannot bring forth evil fruit, neither can a corrupt tree bring forth good fruit.

Every tree that bringeth not forth good fruit is hewn down, and cast into the fire.

Wherefore by their fruits ye shall know them.

MATTHEW 7:15–20

BEHOLD, there went out a sower to sow,

And it came to pass, as he sowed, some fell by the wayside, and the fowls of the air came and devoured it up.

And some fell on stony ground, where it had not much earth; and immediately it sprang up, because it had no depth of earth.

But when the sun was up, it was scorched; and because it had no root, it withered away.

And some fell among thorns, and the thorns grew up, and choked it, and it yielded no fruit.

And other fell on good ground, and did yield fruit that sprang up and increased; and brought forth, some thirty, and some sixty, and some a hundred.

And he said unto them, He that hath ears to hear, let him hear.

MARK 4:4–9

UNTO what is the kingdom of God like? And whereunto shall I resemble it?

It is like a grain of mustard seed, which a man took,

and cast into his garden; and it grew, and waxed a great
tree; and the fowls of the air lodged in the branches of it.

And again he said, Whereunto shall I liken the
kingdom of God?

It is like leaven, which a woman took and hid in three
measures of meal, till the whole was leavened.

LUKE 13:18–21

A certain man had two sons,

And the younger of them said to his father, Father,
give me the portion of goods that falleth to me. And he
divided unto them his living.

And not many days after the younger son gathered all
together, and took his journey into a far country, and there
wasted his substance with riotous living.

And when he had spent all, there arose a mighty
famine in that land; and he began to be in want.

And he went and joined himself to a citizen of that
country; and he sent him into his fields to feed swine.

And he would fain have filled his belly with the husks
that the swine did eat: and no man gave unto him.

And when he came to himself, he said, How many
hired servants of my father's have bread enough and to
spare, and I perish with hunger!

I will arise and go to my father, and will say unto him,
Father, I have sinned against Heaven, and before thee,

And am no more worthy to be called thy son; make
me as one of thy hired servants.

And he arose, and came to his father. But when he was
yet a great way off, his father saw him, and had
compassion, and ran, and fell on his neck, and kissed him.

And the son said unto him, Father, I have sinned
against Heaven, and in thy sight, and am no more worthy
to be called thy son.

But the father said to his servants, Bring forth the best robe, and put it on him; and put a ring on his hand, and shoes on his feet,

And bring hither the fatted calf, and kill it; and let us eat, and be merry,

For this my son was dead, and is alive again; he was lost, and is found. And they began to be merry.

Now his elder son was in the field, and as he came and drew nigh to the house, he heard music and dancing.

And he called one of the servants, and asked what these things meant.

And he said unto him, Thy brother is come; and thy father hath killed the fatted calf, because he hath received him safe and sound.

And he was angry, and would not go in; therefore came his father out, and entreated him.

And he answering said to his father, Lo, these many years do I serve thee, neither transgressed I at any time thy commandment, and yet thou never gavest me a kid, that I might make merry with my friends;

But as soon as this thy son was come, which hath devoured thy living with harlots, thou hast killed for him the fatted calf.

And he said unto him, Son, thou art ever with me, and all that I have is thine.

It was meet that we should make merry, and be glad, for this thy brother was dead, and is alive again; and was lost, and is found.

LUKE 15:11–32

I am the true vine, and my Father is the husbandman.

Every branch in me that beareth not fruit he taketh away; and every branch that beareth fruit, he purgeth it, that it may bring forth more fruit.

Now ye are clean through the word which I have spoken unto you.

Abide in me, and I in you. As the branch cannot bear fruit of itself, except it abide in the vine, no more can ye, except ye abide in me.

I am the vine, ye are the branches: He that abideth in me, and I in him, the same bringeth forth much fruit, for without me ye can do nothing.

If a man abide not in me, he is cast forth as a branch, and is withered; and men gather them, and cast them into the fire, and they are burned.

If ye abide in me, and my words abide in you, ye shall ask what ye will, and it shall be done unto you.

Herein is my Father glorified, that ye bear much fruit; so shall ye be my disciples.

As the Father hath loved me, so have I loved you; continue ye in my love.

If ye keep my commandments, ye shall abide in my love; even as I have kept my Father's commandments, and abide in his love.

These things have I spoken unto you, that my joy might remain in you, and that your joy might be full.

This is my commandment, That ye love one another, as I have loved you.

JOHN 15:1–12

LEAVING the principles of the doctrine of Christ, let us go on unto perfection; not laying again the foundation of repentance from dead works, and of faith toward God,

Of the doctrine of baptisms, and of laying on of hands, and of resurrection of the dead, and of eternal judgment.

And this will we do, if God permit.

For it is impossible for those who were once enlightened, and have tasted of the heavenly gift, and were made partakers of the Holy Ghost,

And have tasted the good word of God, and the powers of the world to come,

If they shall fall away, to renew them again unto repentance; seeing they crucify to themselves the Son of God afresh, and put him to an open shame.

For the earth which drinketh in the rain that cometh oft upon it, and bringeth forth herbs meet for them by whom it is dressed, receiveth blessing from God:

But that which beareth thorns and briers is rejected, and is nigh unto cursing; whose end is to be burned.

But, beloved, we are persuaded better things of you, and things that accompany salvation, though we thus speak.

For God is not unrighteous to forget your work and labor of love, which ye have shewed toward his name, in that ye have ministered to the saints, and do minister.

And we desire that every one of you do shew the same diligence to the full assurance of hope unto the end:

That ye be not slothful, but followers of them who through faith and patience inherit the promises.

For when God made promise to Abraham, because he could swear by no greater, he swore by himself,

Saying, Surely blessing I will bless thee, and multiplying I will multiply thee.

And so, after he had patiently endured, he obtained the promise.

For men verily swear by the greater, and an oath for confirmation is to them an end of all strife.

Wherein God, willing more abundantly to shew unto the heirs of promise the immutability of his counsel, confirmed it by an oath:

That by two immutable things, in which it was impossible for God to lie, we might have a strong consolation, who have fled for refuge to lay hold upon the hope set before us:

Which hope we have as an anchor of the soul, both sure and steadfast . . .

HEBREWS 6:1–20

WHAT doth it profit, my brethren, though a man say he hath faith, and have not works? Can faith save him?

If a brother or sister be naked, and destitute of daily food,

And one of you say unto them, Depart in peace, be ye warmed and filled; notwithstanding ye give them not those things which are needful to the body; what doth it profit?

Even so faith, if it hath not works, is dead, being alone.

Yea, a man may say, Thou hast faith, and I have works; shew me thy faith without thy works, and I will shew thee my faith by my works.

Thou believest that there is one God; thou doest well; the devils also believe, and tremble.

But wilt thou know, O vain man, that faith without works is dead?

Was not Abraham our father justified by works, when he had offered Isaac his son upon the altar?

Seest thou how faith wrought with his works, and by works was faith made perfect?

And the scripture was fulfilled which saith, Abraham believed God, and it was imputed unto him for righteousness; and he was called the Friend of God.

Ye see then how that by works a man is justified, and not by faith only.

Likewise also was not Rahab the harlot justified by works, when she had received the messengers, and had sent them out another way?

For as the body without the spirit is dead, so faith without works is dead also.

JAMES 2:14–26

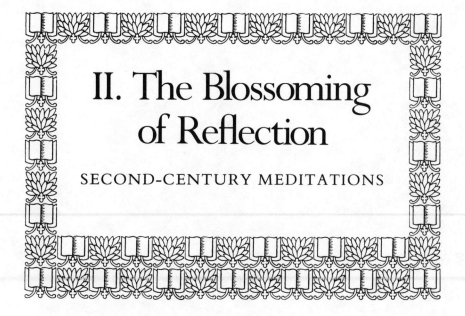

II. The Blossoming of Reflection

SECOND-CENTURY MEDITATIONS

Let us contemplate him with our understanding.

CLEMENT OF ROME

IN the second century, Jewish wisdom traditions (and their New Testament adaptations) are supplemented extensively by forms and styles of discourse stemming from the Greek philosophical schools and later codified in Latin rhetorical practice. With this development, almost all the forms that the earliest Christian meditations take are now firmly established—the epigram or saying, the discourse or dialogue, the exegetical homily, the similitude or extended parable, and the theological essay. What unites them is this: each is intended for repeated contemplation and reflection, with the stated or implicit goal of deepening the Christian's faith by enhancing his or her understanding and by prompting ethical deeds.

All these genres are represented in chapters two and three. In excerpts from his first Epistle, Clement of Rome, bishop at the turn of the second century, combines the teaching and the pastoral office in a simple but moving exhortation to faithfulness. The selection from Barnabas offers for meditation the metaphor of the two ways, which is familiar to readers of the Dead Sea Scrolls. Its asceticism and dualism prefigure that of the later Christian monks. The three similitudes from the Shepherd of Hermas are part of a lengthy revelatory discourse. Finally, the fragments from Justin Martyr and Irenaeus demonstrate the way in which a saying or illustration might be culled by a later theologian from its original context to serve in a new way as an object for reflection.

There is probably no richer early source for Christian meditations than the Nag Hammadi library. Perhaps one reason is that the Gnostics gave knowledge primacy over faith, which made the wisdom tradition, especially in its more esoteric manifestations, a natural font for the expression of their own theology. Choosing among many possibilities, we include here excerpts from a revelatory discourse (*The Dialogue of the Savior*); a theological meditation on Truth (*The Gospel of Truth*—perhaps a meditation on the Gospel of John); and an apology framed as a dialogue (*The Letter to Rheginos*).

If each of these works is decidedly Gnostic in theology, the final two selections, each a catena of moral sayings intended to guide the daily life of the believer, demonstrate how certain meditations could be employed by orthodox and heretic alike. The first, *The Teaching of Silvanus,* combines Stoic ethical teachings with a dualistic theology favored by many moral rigorists. It echos—in form, if not content—the Book of Ecclesiastes and contains nothing odious to orthodox Christianity. The second, *The Sentences of Sextus,* directly contributed to the development of early Christian ethics. It is a collection of non-Christian meditations or wisdom sayings and was very popular among Christians of every theological stripe.

T W O

The Beginnings of the Orthodox Tradition

I

CHRIST is of those who are humble-minded, and not of those who exalt themselves over his flock. Our Lord Jesus Christ, the Scepter of the majesty of God, did not come in the pomp of pride or arrogance, although he might have done so, but in a lowly condition, as the Holy Spirit had declared regarding him. For he says, "Lord, who hath believed our report, and to whom is the arm of the Lord revealed? We have declared our message in his presence: he is, as it were, a child, and like a root in thirsty ground; he has no form nor glory, yea, we saw him, and he had no form nor comeliness; but his form was without eminence, yea, deficient in comparison with the ordinary form of men. He is a man exposed to stripes and suffering, and acquainted with the endurance of grief: for his countenance was turned away; he was despised, and not esteemed. He bears our iniquities, and is in sorrow for our sakes; yet we supposed that on his own account he was exposed to labor, and stripes, and affliction. But he was wounded for our transgressions, and bruised for our iniquities. The chastisement of our peace was upon him, and by his stripes we were healed. All we, like sheep, have gone astray; every man has wandered in his own way; and the Lord has delivered him up for our sins, while he in the midst of his

sufferings openeth not his mouth. He was brought as a
sheep to the slaughter, and as a lamb before her shearer is
dumb, so he openeth not his mouth. In his humiliation his
judgment was taken away; who shall declare his generation?
For his life is taken from the earth. For the transgressions of
my people was he brought down to death. And I will give
the wicked for his sepulcher, and the rich for his death,
because he did no iniquity, neither was guile found in his
mouth. And the Lord is pleased to purify him by stripes. If
ye make an offering for sin, your soul shall see a long-lived
seed. And the Lord is pleased to relieve him of the affliction
of his soul, to show him light, and to form him with
understanding, to justify the Just One who ministereth well
to many; and he himself shall carry their sins. On this
account he shall inherit many, and shall divide the spoil of
the strong; because his soul was delivered to death, and he
was reckoned among the transgressors, and he bare the sins
of many, and for their sins was he delivered." And again he
saith, "I am a worm, and no man; a reproach of men, and
despised of the people. All that see me have derided me;
they have spoken with their lips; they have wagged their
head, saying he hoped in God, let him deliver him, let him
save him, since he delighteth in him." Ye see, beloved,
what is the example which has been given us; for if the
Lord thus humbled himself, what shall we do who have
through him come under the yoke of his grace?

II

The humility and godly submission of so great and
illustrious men have rendered not only us, but also all the
generations before us, better; even as many as have received
his oracles in fear and truth. Wherefore, having so many
great and glorious examples set before us, let us turn again
to the practice of that peace which from the beginning was

the mark set before us; and let us look steadfastly to the Father and Creator of the universe, and cleave to his mighty and surpassingly great gifts and benefactions of peace. Let us contemplate him with our understanding, and look with the eyes of our soul to his long-suffering will. Let us reflect how free from wrath he is toward all his creation.

III

The heavens, revolving under his government, are subject to him in peace. Day and night run the course appointed by him, in no wise hindering each other. The sun and moon, with the companies of the stars, roll on in harmony according to his command, within their prescribed limits, and without any deviation. The fruitful earth, according to his will, brings forth food in abundance, at the proper seasons, for man and beast and all the living beings upon it, never hesitating, nor changing any of the ordinances which he has fixed. The unsearchable places of abysses, and the indescribable arrangements of the lower world, are restrained by the same laws. The vast unmeasurable sea, gathered together by his working into various basins, never passes beyond the bounds placed around it, but does as he has commanded. For he said, "Thus far shalt thou come, and thy waves shall be broken within thee." The ocean, impassable to man, and the worlds beyond it, are regulated by the same enactments of the Lord. The seasons of spring, summer, autumn, and winter peacefully give place to one another. The winds in their several quarters fulfill, at the proper time, their service without hindrance. The ever-flowing fountains, formed both for enjoyment and health, furnish without fail their breasts for the life of men. The very smallest of living beings meet together in peace and concord. All these the great Creator and Lord of all has appointed to exist in peace and harmony; while he does good to all, but most abundantly to us who have fled for refuge to his compassions through Jesus Christ our Lord, to whom be glory and majesty forever and ever. Amen.

IV

Take heed, beloved, lest his many kindnesses lead to the condemnation of us all. For thus it must be unless we walk worthy of him, and with one mind do those things which are good and well-pleasing in his sight. For the Scripture saith in a certain place, "The Spirit of the Lord is a candle searching the secret parts of the belly." Let us reflect how near he is, and that none of the thoughts or reasonings in which we engage are hid from him. It is right, therefore, that we should not leave the post which his will has assigned us. Let us rather offend those men who are foolish, and inconsiderate, and lifted up, and who glory in the pride of their speech, than offend God. Let us reverence the Lord Jesus Christ, whose blood was given for us; let us esteem those who have the rule over us; let us honor the aged among us; let us train up the young men in the fear of God; let us direct our wives to that which is good. Let them exhibit the lovely habit of purity in all their conduct; let them show forth the sincere disposition of meekness; let them make manifest the command which they have of their tongue, by their manner of speaking; let them display their love, not by preferring one to another, but by showing equal affection to all that piously fear God. Let your children be partakers of true Christian training; let them learn of how great avail humility is with God—how much the spirit of pure affection can prevail with him—how excellent and great his fear is, and how it saves all those who walk in it with a pure mind. For he is a Searcher of the thoughts and desires of the heart: his breath is in us; and when he pleases, he will take it away.

V

Let us consider, beloved, how the Lord continually proves to us that there shall be a future resurrection, of which he has rendered the Lord Jesus Christ the firstfruits by raising him from the dead. Let us contemplate, beloved, the resurrection which is at all times taking place. Day and night declare to us a resurrection. The night sinks to sleep, and the day arises; the day again departs, and the night comes on. Let us behold the fruits of the earth, how the sowing of grain takes place. The sower goes forth, and casts it into the ground; and the seed being thus scattered, though dry and naked when it fell upon the earth, is gradually dissolved. Then out of its dissolution the mighty power of the providence of the Lord raises it up again, and from one seed many arise and bring forth fruit.

VI

Let us consider that wonderful sign of the resurrection which takes place in Eastern lands, that is, in Arabia and the countries round about. There is a certain bird which is called a phoenix. This is the only one of its kind, and lives five hundred years. And when the time of its dissolution draws near that it must die, it builds itself a nest of frankincense and myrrh and other spices, into which, when the time is fulfilled, it enters and dies. But as the flesh decays a certain kind of worm is produced, which, being nourished by the juices of the dead bird, brings forth feathers. Then, when it has acquired strength, it takes up that nest in which are the bones of its parent, and bearing these it passes from the land of Arabia into Egypt, to the city called Heliopolis. And, in open day, flying in the sight of all men, it places them on the altar of the sun, and having done this, hastens back to its former abode. The

priests then inspect the registers of the dates, and find that
it has returned exactly as the five hundredth year was
completed.

Do we then deem it any great and wonderful thing for
the Maker of all things to raise up again those that have
piously served him in the assurance of a good faith, when
even by a bird he shows us the mightiness of his power to
fulfill his promise?

VII

How blessed and wonderful, beloved, are the gifts of God!
Life in immortality, splendor in righteousness, truth in
perfect confidence, faith in assurance, self-control in
holiness! And all these fall under the cognizance of our
understandings now; what then shall those things be which
are prepared for such as wait for him? The Creator and
Father of all worlds, the Most Holy, alone knows their
amount and their beauty. Let us therefore earnestly strive to
be found in the number of those that wait for him, in order
that we may share in his promised gifts. But how, beloved,
shall this be done? If our understanding be fixed by faith
toward God; if we earnestly seek the things which are
pleasing and acceptable to him; if we do the things which
are in harmony with his blameless will; and if we follow
the way of truth, casting away from us all unrighteousness
and iniquity, along with all covetousness, strife, evil
practices, deceit, whispering, and evil-speaking, all hatred
of God, pride and haughtiness, vainglory and ambition.
For they that do such things are hateful to God; and not
only they that do them, but also those that take pleasure in
them that do them.

VIII

Let us therefore, with all haste, put an end to this state of things; and let us fall down before the Lord, and beseech him with tears, that he would mercifully be reconciled to us, and restore us to our former seemly and holy practice of brotherly love. For such conduct is the gate of righteousness, which is set open for the attainment of life, as it is written, "Open to me the gates of righteousness; I will go in by them, and will praise the Lord; this is the gate of the Lord: the righteous shall enter in by it." Although, therefore, many gates have been set open, yet this gate of righteousness is that gate in Christ by which blessed are all they that have entered in and have directed their way in holiness and righteousness, doing all things without disorder. Let a man be faithful; let him be powerful in the utterance of knowledge; let him be wise in judging of words; let him be pure in all his deeds; yet the more he seems to be superior to others in these respects, the more humble-minded ought he to be, and to seek the common good of all, and not merely his own advantage.

IX

Let him who has love in Christ keep the commandments of Christ. Who can describe the blessed bond of the love of God? What man is able to tell the excellence of its beauty, as it ought to be told? The height to which love exalts is unspeakable. Love unites us to God. Love covers a multitude of sins. Love beareth all things, is long-suffering in all things. There is nothing base, nothing arrogant in love. Love admits of no schisms; love gives rise to no seditions; love does all things in harmony. By love have all the elect of God been made perfect; without love nothing is

Flagstaff Public Library
Flagstaff, Arizona

well-pleasing to God. In love has the Lord taken us to himself. On account of the love he bore us, Jesus Christ our Lord gave his blood for us by the will of God; his flesh for our flesh, and his soul for our souls.

X

Ye see, beloved, how great and wonderful a thing is love, and that there is no declaring its perfection. Who is fit to be found in it, except such as God has vouchsafed to render so? Let us pray, therefore, and implore of his mercy, that we may live blameless in love, free from all human partialities for one above another. All the generations from Adam even unto this day have passed away; but those who, through the grace of God, have been made perfect in love, now possess a place among the godly, and shall be made manifest at the revelation of the kingdom of Christ. For it is written, "Enter into thy secret chambers for a little time, until my wrath and fury pass away; and I will remember a propitious day, and will raise you up out of your graves." Blessed are we, beloved, if we keep the commandments of God in the harmony of love; that so through love our sins may be forgiven us.

THE FIRST EPISTLE OF CLEMENT

THERE are two ways of doctrine and authority, the one of light, and the other of darkness. But there is a great difference between these two ways. For over one are stationed the light-bringing angels of God, but over the other the angels of Satan. And God is Lord for ever and ever, but Satan is prince of the time of iniquity.

The way of light is as follows. If anyone desires to travel to the appointed place, he must be zealous in his works. The knowledge, which is given to us for the purpose of walking in this way, is the following. Thou shalt love him that created thee; thou shalt glorify him that redeemed thee from death. Thou shalt be simple in heart, and rich in spirit. Thou shalt not join thyself to those who walk in the way of death. Thou shalt hate doing what is unpleasing to God; thou shalt hate all hypocrisy. Thou shalt not forsake the commandments of the Lord. Thou shalt not exalt thyself, but shalt be of a lowly mind. Thou shalt not take glory to thyself. Thou shalt not take evil counsel against thy neighbor. Thou shalt not allow overboldness to enter into thy soul. Thou shalt not commit fornication; thou shalt not commit adultery; thou shalt not be a corrupter of youth. Thou shalt not let the word of God issue from thy lips with any kind of impurity. Thou shalt not accept persons when thou reprovest anyone for transgression. Thou shalt be meek; thou shalt be peaceable. Thou shalt tremble at the words which thou hearest. Thou shalt not be mindful of evil against thy brother. Thou shalt not be of doubtful mind as to whether a thing shall be or not. Thou shalt not take the name of the Lord in vain. Thou shalt love thy neighbor more than thine own soul. Thou shalt not slay the child by procuring abortion; nor, again, shalt thou destroy it after it is born. Thou shalt not withdraw thy hand from thy son, or from thy daughter, but from their infancy thou shalt teach them the fear of the Lord. Thou shalt not covet what is thy neighbor's, nor shalt thou be avaricious. Thou shalt not be joined in soul with the haughty, but thou shalt be reckoned with the righteous and lowly. Receive thou as good things the trials which come upon thee. Thou shalt not be of double mind or of double tongue, for a double tongue is a snare of death. Thou shalt be subject to the Lord, and to other masters as the image of God, with modesty and fear. Thou shalt not issue orders with bitterness to thy maidservant or thy manservant, who trust in the same God, lest thou shouldst not reverence that God who is above both; for he came to call men not according to their outward appearance, but according as the Spirit had prepared them. Thou shalt communicate in all things with thy neighbor; thou shalt not call things thine own; for if ye are partakers in common of things which are incorruptible, how much more should you be of those things which are corruptible! Thou shalt not be hasty with thy tongue, for the mouth is a snare of death. As far as possible, thou shalt be pure in thy soul. Do not be ready to stretch forth thy hands to take, whilst thou contractest them to give. Thou shalt love, as the apple of thine eye, every one that speaketh to thee the word of the Lord. Thou shalt remember the day of judgment, night and day. Thou shalt seek out every day the faces of the saints, either by word examining them, and going to exhort them, and meditating how to save a soul by the word, or by thy hands thou shalt labor for the redemption of thy sins. Thou shalt not hesitate to give, nor murmur when thou givest. "Give to everyone that asketh thee," and thou shalt know who is the good Recompenser of the reward. Thou shalt preserve what thou hast received in charge, neither adding to it nor taking from it. To the last thou shalt hate the wicked one. Thou shalt judge righteously. Thou shalt not make a schism, but thou shalt pacify those that contend by bringing them together. Thou shalt confess thy sins. Thou shalt not go to prayer with an evil conscience. This is the way of light.

But the way of darkness is crooked, and full of cursing; for it is the way of eternal death with punishment, in which way are the things that destroy the soul, namely, idolatry, overconfidence, the arrogance of power, hypocrisy, double-heartedness, adultery, murder, rapine, haughtiness, transgression, deceit, malice, self-sufficiency, poisoning, magic, avarice, want of the fear of God. In this way, too, are those who persecute the good, those who hate truth, those who love falsehood, those who know not the reward of righteousness, those who cleave not to that which is good, those who attend not with just judgment to the widow and orphan, those who watch not to the fear of God, but incline to wickedness, from whom meekness and patience are far off; persons who love vanity, follow after a reward, pity not the needy, labor not in aid of him who is overcome with toil; who are prone to evil-speaking, who know not him that made them, who are murderers of children, destroyers of the workmanship of God; who turn away him that is in want, who oppress the afflicted, who are advocates of the rich, who are unjust judges of the poor, and who are in every respect transgressors.

It is well, therefore, that he who has learned the judgments of the Lord, as many as have been written, should walk in them. For he who keepeth these shall be glorified in the kingdom of God; but he who chooseth other things shall be destroyed with his works.

THE EPISTLE OF BARNABAS

I

As I was walking in the field, and observing an elm and vine, and determining in my own mind respecting them and their fruits, the Shepherd appears to me, and says, "What is it that you are thinking about the elm and vine?" "I am considering," I reply, "that they become each other exceedingly well." "These two trees," he continues, "are intended as an example for the servants of God." "I would like to know," said I, "the example which these trees, you say, are intended to teach." "Do you see," he says, "the

elm and the vine?" "I see them, sir," I replied. "This vine,"
he continued, "produces fruit, and the elm is an unfruitful
tree; but unless the vine be trained upon the elm, it cannot
bear much fruit when extended at length upon the ground;
and the fruit which it does bear is rotten, because the plant
is not suspended upon the elm. When, therefore, the vine is
cast upon the elm, it yields fruit both from itself and from
the elm. You see, moreover, that the elm also produces
much fruit, not less than the vine, but even more; because,"
he continued, "the vine, when suspended upon the elm,
yields much fruit, and good; but when thrown upon the
ground, what it produces is small and rotten. This
similitude, therefore, is for the servants of God—for the
poor man and for the rich." "How so, sir?" said I; "explain
the matter to me." "Listen," he said: "The rich man has
much wealth, but is poor in matters relating to the Lord,
because he is distracted about his riches; and he offers very
few confessions and intercessions to the Lord, and those
which he does offer are small and weak, and have no power
above. But when the rich man refreshes the poor, and
assists him in his necessities, believing that what he does
to the poor man will be able to find its reward with
God—because the poor man is rich in intercession and
confession, and his intercession has great power with
God—then the rich man helps the poor in all things
without hesitation; and the poor man, being helped by the
rich, intercedes for him, giving thanks to God for him who
bestows gifts upon him. And he still continues to interest
himself zealously for the poor man, that his wants may be
constantly supplied. For he knows that the intercession of
the poor man is acceptable and influential with God. Both,
accordingly, accomplish their work. The poor man makes
intercession; a work in which he is rich, which he received
from the Lord, and with which he recompenses the master
who helps him. And the rich man, in like manner,
unhesitatingly bestows upon the poor man the riches which

he received from the Lord. And this is a great work, and acceptable before God, because he understands the object of his wealth, and has given to the poor of the gifts of the Lord, and rightly discharged his service to him. Among men, however, the elm appears not to produce fruit, and they do not know nor understand that if a drought come, the elm, which contains water, nourishes the vine; and the vine, having an unfailing supply of water, yields double fruit both for itself and for the elm. So also poor men interceding with the Lord on behalf of the rich, increase their riches; and the rich, again, aiding the poor in their necessities, satisfy their souls. Both, therefore, are partners in the righteous work. He who does these things shall not be deserted by God, but shall be enrolled in the books of the living. Blessed are they who have riches, and who understand that they are from the Lord. For they who are of that mind will be able to do some good."

II

He showed me many trees having no leaves, but withered, as it seemed to me; for all were alike. And he said to me, "Do you see those trees?" "I see, sir," I replied, "that all are alike, and withered." He answered me, and said, "These trees which you see are those who dwell in this world." "Why, then, sir," I said, "are they withered, as it were, and alike?" "Because," he said, "neither are the righteous manifest in this life, nor sinners, but they are alike; for this life is a winter to the righteous, and they do not manifest themselves, because they dwell with sinners: for as in winter trees that have cast their leaves are alike, and it is not seen which are dead and which are living, so in this world neither do the righteous show themselves, nor sinners, but all are alike one to another."

III

He showed me again many trees, some budding, and others withered. And he said to me, "Do you see these trees?" "I see, sir," I replied, "some putting forth buds, and others withered." "Those," he said, "which are budding are the righteous who are to live in the world to come; for the coming world is the summer of the righteous, but the winter of sinners. When, therefore, the mercy of the Lord shines forth, then shall they be made manifest who are the servants of God, and all men shall be made manifest. For as in summer the fruits of each individual tree appear, and it is ascertained of what sort they are, so also the fruits of the righteous shall be manifest, and all who have been fruitful in that world shall be made known. But the heathen and sinners, like the withered trees which you saw, will be found to be those who have been withered and unfruitful in that world, and shall be burnt as wood, and so made manifest, because their actions were evil during their lives. For the sinners shall be consumed because they sinned and did not repent, and the heathen shall be burned because they knew not him who created them. Do you therefore bear fruit, that in that summer your fruit may be known. And refrain from much business, and you will never sin; for they who are occupied with much business commit also many sins, being distracted about their affairs, and not at all serving their Lord. How, then," he continued, "can such a one ask and obtain anything from the Lord, if he serve him not? . . . And in the performance even of a single action a man can serve the Lord; for his mind will not be perverted from the Lord, but he will serve him, having a pure mind. If, therefore, you do these things, you shall be able to bear fruit for the life to come. And everyone who will do these things shall bear fruit."

SIMILITUDES FROM THE SHEPHERD OF HERMAS

I

WE shall not injure God by remaining ignorant of him, but shall deprive ourselves of his friendship.

II

The unskillfulness of the teacher proves destructive to his disciples, and the carelessness of the disciples entails danger on the teacher, and especially should they owe their negligence to his want of knowledge.

III

As it is inherent in all bodies formed by God to have a shadow, so it is fitting that God, who is just, should render to those who choose what is good, and to those who prefer what is evil, to everyone according to his deserts.

IV

Neither shall light ever be darkness as long as light exists, nor shall the truth of the things pertaining to us be controverted. For truth is that than which nothing is more powerful. Everyone who might speak the truth, and speaks it not, shall be judged by God.

V

Sound doctrine does not enter into the hard and disobedient heart; but, as if beaten back, enters anew into itself.

VI

As the good of the body is health, so the good of the soul is knowledge, which is indeed a kind of health of soul, by which a likeness to God is attained.

VII

To yield and give way to our passions is the lowest slavery, even as to rule over them is the only liberty.

The greatest of all good is to be free from sin, the next is to be justified; but he must be reckoned the most unfortunate of men, who, while living unrighteously, remains for a long time unpunished.

Animals in harness cannot but be carried over a precipice by the inexperience and badness of their driver, even as by his skillfulness and excellence they will be saved.

The end contemplated by a philosopher is likeness to God, so far as that is possible.

FRAGMENTS FROM THE WRITINGS OF JUSTIN MARTYR

I

As long as anyone has the means of doing good to his neighbors, and does not do so, he shall be reckoned a stranger to the love of the Lord.

II

The will and the energy of God is the effective and foreseeing cause of every time and place and age, and of every nature. The will is the reason of the intellectual soul, which is within us, inasmuch as it is the faculty belonging to it which is endowed with freedom of action. The will is the mind desiring some object and an appetite possessed of intelligence, yearning after that thing which is desired.

III

Since God is vast, and the Architect of the world, and omnipotent, he created things that reach to immensity both by the Architect of the world and by an omnipotent will, and with a new effect, potently and efficaciously, in order that the entire fullness of those things which have been produced might come into being, although they had no previous existence—that is, whatever does not fall under our observation, and also what lies before our eyes. And so does he contain all things in particular, and leads them on to their own proper result, on account of which they were called into being and produced, in no way changed into anything else than what it (the end) had originally been by nature. For this is the property of the working of God, not merely to proceed to the infinitude of the understanding, or even to overpass our powers of mind, reason and speech, time and place, and every age; but also to go beyond substance, and fullness or perfection.

IV

The business of the Christian is nothing else than to be ever preparing for death.

V

We therefore have formed the belief that our bodies also do rise again. For although they go to corruption, yet they do not perish; for the earth, receiving the remains, preserves them, even like fertile seed mixed with more fertile ground. Again, as a bare grain is sown, and, germinating by the command of God its Creator, rises again, clothed upon and glorious, but not before it has died and suffered decomposition, and become mingled with the earth; so it is seen from this, that we have not entertained a vain belief in the resurrection of the body. But although it is dissolved at the appointed time, because of the primeval disobedience, it is placed, as it were, in the crucible of the earth, to be recast again; not then as this corruptible body, but pure, and no longer subject to decay, so that to each body its own soul shall be restored; and when it is clothed upon with this, it shall not experience sorrow, but shall rejoice, continuing permanently in a state of purity, having for its companion a just consort, not an insidious one, possessing in every respect the things pertaining to it, it shall receive these with perfect accuracy; it shall not receive bodies diverse from what they had been, nor delivered from suffering or disease, nor as rendered glorious, but as they departed this life, in sins or in righteous actions: and such as they were, such shall they be clothed with upon resuming life; and such as they were in unbelief, such shall they be faithfully judged.

VI

Know thou that every man is either empty or full. For if he has not the Holy Spirit, he has no knowledge of the Creator; he has not received Jesus Christ the Life; he knows not the Father who is in Heaven; if he does not live after the dictates of reason, after the heavenly law, he is not a sober-minded person, nor does he act uprightly: such a one is empty. If, on the other hand, he receives God, who says, "I will dwell with them, and walk in them, and I will be their God," such a one is not empty, but full.

VII

Christ, who was called the Son of God before the ages, was manifested in the fullness of time, in order that he might cleanse us through his blood, who were under the power of sin, presenting us as pure sons to his Father, if we yield ourselves obediently to the chastisement of the Spirit. And in the end of time he shall come to do away with all evil, and to reconcile all things, in order that there may be an end of all impurities.

VIII

Speaking always well of the worthy, but never ill of the unworthy, we also shall attain to the glory and kingdom of God.

IX

It is not an easy thing for a soul, under the influence of error, to be persuaded of the contrary opinion.

FRAGMENTS FROM THE WRITINGS OF IRENAEUS

THREE

Meditations from
Nag Hammadi

I

THE Savior said to his disciples, "Already the time has come, brothers, that we should leave behind our labor and stand in the rest; for he who stands in the rest will rest forever.

II

His disciples said, "Lord, who is the one who seeks and who is the one who reveals?"

The Lord said, "The one who seeks is also the one who reveals."

Matthew said, "Lord, who is the one who speaks and who is the one who hears?"

The Lord said, "The one who speaks is also the one who hears, and the one who sees is also the one who reveals."

Mariam said, "O Lord, behold, when I am bearing the body, for what reason do I weep, and for what reason do I laugh?"

The Lord said, "If you weep because of its deeds you will abide, and the mind laughs. . . . If one does not stand in the darkness, he will not be able to see the light. . . .

III

Matthew said, "Lord, I wish to see that place of life, that place in which there is no evil, but rather it is the pure light."

The Lord said, "Brother Matthew, you cannot see it, as long you wear the flesh."

Matthew said, "O Lord, even if I can not see it, let me know it."

The Lord said, "Every one of you who has known himself has seen it; everything that is fitting for him to do, he does it. And he has been doing it in his goodness."

"As for those who speak out of joy and truth, you are in their heart. And if he comes from the body of the Father through men, and they do not receive him, he turns again to his place. He who knows not the works of perfection knows nothing. If one does not stand in the darkness, he will not be able to see the light. If one does not understand how the fire came to be, he will burn in it, because he does not know his root. If one does not first understand the water, he does not know anything. For what is the use for him to receive baptism in it? If one does not understand how the wind that blows came to be, he will run with it. If one does not understand how the body that he wears came to be, he will perish with it. And he who does not know the Son, how will he know the Father? And he who will not know the root of all things, they (all things) are hidden from him. He who will not know the root of wickedness is not a stranger to it. He who will not understand how he came will not understand how he will go, and is not a stranger to this world which will perish and which will be humbled."

IV

Matthew said, "Why do we not put ourselves to rest at once?"

The Lord said, "You will when you lay down these burdens."

Matthew said, "In what way does the little one cleave to the great one?"

The Lord said, "When you leave behind you the things that will not be able to follow you, then you will put yourselves to rest."

Mariam said, "I want to know how all things exist."

The Lord said, "Whoever seeks life knows this, for this is their wealth. For the enjoyment of this world is a lie, and its gold and its silver is error."

His disciples said to him, "What shall we do in order that our work may be perfect?"

The Lord said to them, "Be prepared before the All. Blessed is the man who has found the interpretation about this thought, the struggle with his eyes. He did not kill nor was he killed, but he came forth victorious."

Judas said, "Tell me, Lord, what is the beginning of the way?"

He said, "Love and goodness. For if there had been one of these dwelling with the archons, wickedness would never have come to be."

Matthew said, "O Lord, you have spoken without pain of the end of the All."

The Lord said, "Everything which I have said to you you have understood and received in faith. If you have known them, they are yours; if not, they are not yours."

They said to him, "What is the place to which we shall go?"

The Lord said, "The place which you can reach, stand there!"

Mariam said, "Is everything that is established seen in this way?"

The Lord said, "I have told you that he who sees is he who reveals."

THE DIALOGUE OF THE SAVIOR

JUST as there lies hidden in a will, before it is opened, the fortune of the deceased master of the house, so it is with the all, which lay hidden while the Father of the all was invisible, the one who is from himself, from whom all spaces come forth. For this reason Jesus appeared; he was nailed to a tree; he published the edict of the Father on the cross. O such great teaching! He draws himself down to death though life eternal clothes him. Having stripped himself of the perishable rags, he put on imperishability, which no one can possibly take away from him. Having entered the empty spaces of terrors, he passed through those who were stripped naked by oblivion, being knowledge and perfection, proclaiming the things that are in the heart of the Father in order to teach those who will receive teaching. . . .

His wisdom contemplates the Word, his teaching utters it, his knowledge has revealed it. His forbearance is a crown upon it, his gladness is in harmony with it, his glory has exalted it, his image has revealed it, his repose has received it into itself, his love has made a body over it, his fidelity has embraced it. In this way the Word of the Father goes forth in the all, as the fruit of his heart and an impression of his will. But it supports the all; it chooses it and also receives the impression of the all, purifying it, bringing it back into the Father, into the Mother, Jesus of the infiniteness of gentleness.

THE GOSPEL OF TRUTH

THIS is the perfection in the thought of the Father, and these are the words of his meditation. Each one of his words is the work of his one will in the revelation of his Word. While they were still in the depth of his thought, the Word which was first to come forth revealed them along with a mind that speaks the one Word in silent grace. It was called thought since they were in it before being revealed. It came about, then, that it was first to come forth at the time that was pleasing to the will of him who willed. And the will is what the Father rests in and is pleased with. Nothing happens without him, nor does anything happen without the will of the Father, but his will is incomprehensible. His trace is the will, and no one will know it, nor is it possible for one to scrutinize it in order to grasp it. But when he wills, what he wills is this—even if the sight does not please them in any way—before God it is the will, the Father. For he knows the beginning of all of them and their end. For at their end he will question them directly. Now the end is receiving knowledge about the one who is hidden, and this is the Father, from whom the beginning came forth, to whom all will return who have come forth from him. And they have appeared for the glory and the joy of his name.

THE GOSPEL OF TRUTH

SOME there are, my son Rheginos, who desire to learn much. They have this aim when they are occupied with questions which lack their answer; and if they succeed with these, they customarily think very highly of themselves. But I do not think they have stood within the Word of Truth. Rather, they seek their own Rest, which we have received through our Savior, our Lord Christ. We received it after we had known the Truth and rested ourselves upon it. But because you ask us pleasantly what is proper concerning the resurrection, I am writing you to say that it is necessary. To be sure many are lacking faith in it, but there are a few who find it. So then, let us discuss the matter. How did the Lord make use of things while existing in flesh and after he had revealed himself as Son of God? He lived in this place where you remain, speaking about the Law of Nature. But I call it "Death." Now the Son of God, Rheginos, was Son of Man. He embraced both of them, possessing the humanity and the divinity, so that on the one hand he might conquer death through his being Son of God, and that on the other through the Son of Man the restoration to the pleroma might occur because originally he was from above, a seed of Truth before this structure had come into being. In this structure many dominions and deities came into existence.

I know I am giving the solution in difficult things, but there is nothing difficult in the Word of Truth. But since the solution appeared so as not to leave anything hidden, but to reveal all things openly concerning existence—the destruction of evil on the one hand but the revelation of the Elect on the other—this is the emanation of Truth and Spirit. Grace is of Truth. The Savior swallowed up death. . . . For he put aside the world which is perishing. He transformed himself into an imperishable Aeon and raised himself up, having swallowed the visible by the invisible, and he gave us the way of our immortality. Then, indeed, as the apostle said, "We suffered with him, and we arose with him, and we went to Heaven with him." Now if we are revealed in this world wearing him, we are that one's beams and we are enclosed by him until our setting, that is to say, our death in this life. We are drawn to Heaven by him like the beams by the sun, not being restrained by anything.

THE LETTER TO RHEGINOS

I

ABOLISH every childish time of life, acquire for yourself strength of mind and soul, and intensify the struggle against every folly of the passions of love and base wickedness, and love of praise, and fondness of contention, and tiresome jealousy and wrath, and anger and the desire of avarice. Guard your camp and weapons and spears. Arm yourself and all the soldiers which are the words, and the commanders which are the counsels, and your mind as a guiding principle.

My son, throw every robber out of your gates. Guard all your gates with torches which are the words, and you will acquire all these things for a quiet life. But he who will not guard these things will become like a city which is desolate since it has been captured, and all kinds of wild beasts have trampled upon it. For thoughts which are not good are evil wild beasts. And your city will be filled with robbers, and you will not be able to acquire peace, but only all kinds of savage wild beasts. The Wicked One, who is a tyrant, is lord over these. While directing this, he is beneath the great mire. The whole city which is your soul will perish.

Remove all these, O wretched soul. Bring in your guide and your teacher. The mind is the guide, but reason is the teacher. They will bring you out of destruction and dangers.

Listen, my son, to my advice! Do not show your back to your enemies and flee, but rather pursue them as a strong one. Be not an animal, with men pursuing you; but rather, be a man, with you pursuing the evil wild beasts, lest somehow they become victorious over you and trample upon you as on a dead man, and you perish due to their wickedness.

O wretched man, what will you do if you fall into their hands? Protect yourself lest you be delivered into the hands of your enemies. Entrust yourself to this pair of friends, reason and mind, and no one will be victorious over you. May God dwell in your camp, may his Spirit protect your gates, and may the mind of divinity protect the walls. Let holy reason become a torch in your mind, burning the wood which is the entirety of sin.

And if you do these things, O my son, you will be victorious over all your enemies, and they will not be able to wage war against you, neither will they be able to stand firm, nor will they be able to get in your way. For if you find these, you will despise them as deniers of truth. They will speak with you, cajoling you and enticing you, not because they are afraid of you, but because they are afraid of those who dwell within you, namely, the guardians of the divinity and the teaching. . . .

II

My son, listen to my teaching which is good and useful, and end the sleep which weighs heavy upon you. Depart from the forgetfulness which fills you with darkness, since if you were unable to do anything, I would not have said these things to you. But Christ came in order to give you this gift. Why do you pursue the darkness though the light is at your disposal? Why do you drink stale water though sweet is available for you? Wisdom summons you, yet you desire folly. Not by your own desire do you do these things, but it is the animal nature within you that does them.

Wisdom summons you in her goodness, saying, "Come to me, all of you, O foolish ones, that you may receive a gift, the understanding which is good and excellent. I am giving to you a high-priestly garment which is woven from every kind of wisdom." What else is evil death except ignorance? What else is evil darkness except familiarity with forgetfulness? Cast your anxiety upon God alone. Do not become desirous of gold and silver which are profitless, but clothe yourself with wisdom like a robe, put knowledge upon you like a crown, and be seated upon a throne of perception. For these are yours, and you will receive them again on high another time.

For a foolish man puts on folly like a robe, and like a garment of sorrow he puts on shame. And he crowns himself with ignorance and takes his seat upon a throne of nescience. For while he is without reason, he leads only himself astray, for he is guided by ignorance. And he goes the ways of the desire of every passion. He swims in the desires of life and has foundered. To be sure, he thinks that he finds profit when he does all the things which are without profit. The wretched man who goes through all these things will die because he does not have the mind, the helmsman. But he is like a ship which the wind tosses to and fro, and like a loose horse which has no rider. For this man needed the rider which is reason. For the wretched one went astray since he did not want advice. He was thrown to and fro by these three evil things: he acquired for himself death as a father, ignorance as a mother, and evil counsels—he acquired them as friends and brothers. Therefore, foolish one, you should mourn for yourself.

From now on, then, my son, return to your divine nature. Cast from you these evil, deceiving friends! Accept Christ, this true friend, as a good teacher. Cast from you death, which has become a father to you. For death did not exist, nor will it exist at the end.

But since you cast from yourself God, the holy Father, the true Life, the Spring of Life, therefore you have obtained death as a father and have acquired ignorance as a mother. They have robbed you of the true knowledge.

But return, my son, to your first father, God, and Wisdom your mother, from whom you came into being from the very first in order that you might fight against all of your enemies, the powers of the Adversary.

Listen, my son, to my advice. Do not be arrogant in opposition to every good opinion, but take for yourself the side of the divinity of reason. Keep the holy commandments of Jesus Christ, and you will reign over every place on earth and will be honored by the angels and the archangels. Then you will acquire them as friends and fellow servants, and you will acquire places in Heaven above.

Do not bring grief and trouble to the divine which is within you. But when you will care for it, will request of it that you remain pure, and will become self-controlled in your soul and body, you will become a throne of wisdom and one belonging to God's household. He will give you a great light through it.

III

Do not allow yourself to be defiled by strange kinds of knowledge. Certainly you know that the schemes of the Adversary are not few and that the tricks which he has are varied? . . . For it is fitting for you to be in agreement with the intelligence of these two: with the intelligence of the snake and with the innocence of the dove—lest he come into you in the guise of a flatterer, as a true friend, saying, "I advise good things for you."

But you did not recognize the deceitfulness of this one when you received him as a true friend. For he casts into your heart evil thoughts as good ones, and hypocrisy in the guise of firm intelligence, avidity in the guise of frugality, love of glory in the guise of that which is beautiful, boastfulness and pride in the guise of great austerity, and godlessness as great godliness. For he who says, "I have many gods," is godless. And he casts spurious knowledge into your heart in the guise of mysterious words. Who will be able to comprehend his thoughts and devices, which are varied, since he is a Great Mind for those who wish to accept him as king?

My son, how will you be able to comprehend the schemes of this one or his soul-killing counsel? For his devices and the schemes of his wickedness are many. And think about his entrances, that is, how he will enter your soul and in what garment he will enter you.

Accept Christ, who is able to set you free, and who has taken on the devices of that one so that through these he might destroy him by deceit. For this is the king whom you have who is forever invincible, against whom no one will be able to fight nor say a word. This is your king and your father, for there is no one like him. The divine teacher is with you always. He is a helper, and he meets you because of the good which is in you.

Do not put maliciousness in your judgment, for every malicious man harms his heart. For only a foolish man goes to his destruction, but a wise man knows his path.

And a foolish man does not guard against speaking a mystery. A wise man, however, does not blurt out every word, but he will be discriminating toward those who hear. Do not mention everything in the presence of those whom you do not know.

Have a great number of friends, but not counselors. First, examine your counselor, for do not honor anyone who flatters. Their word, to be sure, is sweet as honey, but their heart is full of hellebore. For whenever they think that they have become a reliable friend, then they will deceitfully turn against you, and they will cast you down into the mire. . . .

IV

Live with Christ, and he will save you. For he is the true light and the sun of life. For just as the sun which is manifest and makes light for the eyes of the flesh, so Christ illuminates every mind and the heart. For if a wicked man who is in the body has an evil death, how much more so does he who has his mind blind. For every blind man goes along in such a way that he is seen just as one who does not have his mind sane. He does not delight in acquiring the light of Christ, which is reason.

For everything which is manifest is a copy of that which is hidden. For as a fire which burns in a place without being confined to it, so it is with the sun which is in Heaven, all of whose rays extend to places on the earth. Similarly, Christ has a single being, and he gives light to every place. This is also the way in which he speaks of our mind, as if it were a lamp which burns and lights up the place. Being in a part of the soul, it gives light to all the parts. . . .

V

Consider these things about God: he is in every place; on the other hand, he is in no place. With respect to power, to be sure, he is in every place; but with respect to divinity, he is in no place. So, then, it is possible to know God a little. With respect to his power, he fills every place, but in the exaltation of his divinity nothing contains him. Everything is in God, but God is not in anything.

Now what is it to know God? God is all which is in the truth. But it is as impossible to look at Christ as at the sun. God sees everyone; no one looks at him. But Christ without being jealous receives and gives. He is the Light of the Father, as he gives light without being jealous. In this manner he gives light to every place.

And all is Christ, he who has inherited all from the Existent One. For Christ is all, apart from his incorruptibility. For if you consider sin, it is not a reality. For Christ is the idea of incorruptibility, and he is the Light which is shining undefiled. For the sun shines on every impure place, and yet it is not defiled. So it is with Christ: even if he is in the deficiency, yet he is without deficiency. And even if he has been begotten, he is still unbegotten. So it is with Christ: if, on the one hand, he is comprehensible, on the other he is incomprehensible with respect to his actual being. Christ is all. He who does not possess all is unable to know Christ. . . .

And understand by this that he who is in darkness will not be able to see anything unless he receives the light. . . . Examine yourself to see whether you actually have the light, so that if you ask about these things, you may understand how you will escape. For many are seeking in darkness, and they grope about, wishing to understand since there is no light for them.

VI

My son, do not allow your mind to stare downward, but rather let it look by means of the light at things above. For the light will always come from above. Even if the mind is upon the earth, let it seek to pursue the things above. Enlighten your mind with the light of Heaven so that you may turn to the light of Heaven.

Do not tire of knocking on the door of reason, and do not cease walking in the way of Christ. Walk in it so that you may receive rest from your labors. If you walk in another way, there will be no profit in it. For also those who walk in the broad way will go down at their end to the perdition of the mire. For the Underworld is open wide for the soul, and the place of perdition is broad. Accept Christ, the narrow way. For he is oppressed and bears affliction for your sin. . . .

But you, on the other hand, with difficulty give your basic choice to him with a hint that he may take you up with joy! Now the basic choice, which is humility of heart, is the gift of Christ. A contrite heart is the acceptable sacrifice. If you humble yourself, you will be greatly exalted. And if you exalt yourself, you will be exceedingly humbled.

VII

The Tree of Life is Christ. He is Wisdom; he is also the Word. He is the Life, the Power, and the Door. He is the Light, the Messenger, and the Good Shepherd. Entrust yourself to this one who became all for your sake.

Knock on yourself as upon a door, and walk upon yourself as on a straight road. For if you walk on the road, it is impossible for you to go astray. And if you knock with Wisdom, you knock on hidden treasuries.

For since Christ is Wisdom, he makes the foolish man wise. Wisdom is a holy kingdom and a shining robe. For it is much gold which gives you great honor. The Wisdom of God became a type of fool for you so that it might take you up, O foolish one, and make you a wise man. And the Life died for you when Christ was powerless, so that through his death he might give life to you who have died.

Entrust yourself to reason and remove yourself from animalism. For the animal which has no reason is made manifest. For many think that they have reason, but if you look at them attentively, their speech is animalistic.

Give yourself gladness from the true vine of Christ. Satisfy yourself with the true wine in which there is no drunkenness nor error. For the true wine marks the end of drinking since there is in it the power to give joy to the soul and the mind through the Spirit of God. But first, nurture your reasoning powers before you drink of it.

Do not pierce yourself with the sword of sin. Do not burn yourself, O wretched one, with the fire of lust. Do not surrender yourself to barbarians like a prisoner, nor to savage beasts which wish to trample upon you. For they are as lions which roar very loudly. Be not dead lest they trample upon you. You shall be man! It is possible for you through reasoning to conquer them.

But the man who does nothing is unworthy of being called rational man. The rational man is he who fears God. He who fears God does nothing insolent.

VIII

Know who Christ is, and acquire him as a friend, for this is the friend who is faithful. He is also God and Teacher. This one, being God, became man for your sake. It is this one who broke the iron bars of the Underworld and the bronze bolts. It is this one who attacked and cast down every haughty tyrant. It is he who loosened from himself the chains of which he had taken hold. He brought up the poor from the Abyss and the mourners from the Underworld. It is he who humbled the haughty powers; he who put to shame haughtiness through humility; he who has cast down the strong and the boaster through weakness; he who in his contempt scorned that which is considered an honor so that humility for God's sake might be highly exalted; (and) he who has put on humanity. . . .

He is a light from the power of God, and he is an emanation of the pure glory of the Almighty. He is the spotless mirror of the working of God, and he is the image of his goodness. For he is also the light of the Eternal Light. He is the eye which looks at the invisible Father, always serving and forming by the Father's will. He alone was begotten by the Father's good pleasure. For he is an incomprehensible Word, and he is Wisdom and Life. He gives life to and nourishes all living things and powers. Just as the soul gives life to all the members, he rules all with power and gives life to them. For he is the beginning and the end of everyone, watching over all and encompassing them. He is troubled on behalf of everyone, and he rejoices and also mourns. On the one hand, he mourns for those who have been appointed to the place of punishment; on the other, he is troubled about everyone whom he arduously brings to instruction. But he rejoices over everyone who is in purity.

IX

There is no other one hidden except God alone. But he is revealed to everyone, and yet he is very hidden. He is revealed because God knows all. And if they do not wish to affirm it, they will be corrected by their heart. Now he is hidden because no one perceives the things of God. For it is incomprehensible and unsearchable to know the counsel of God. Furthermore, it is difficult to comprehend him and to find Christ. For he is the one who dwells in every place and also in no place. For no one who wants to will be able to know God as he actually is, nor Christ, nor the Spirit, nor the chorus of angels, nor even the archangels, and the thrones of the spirits, and the exalted lordships, and the Great Mind. If you do not know yourself, you will not be able to know all of these.

X

Open the door for yourself that you may know what is.
Knock on yourself that the Word may open for you. For he
is the Ruler of Faith and the Sharp Sword, having become
all for everyone because he wishes to have mercy on
everyone.

My son, prepare yourself to escape from the world
rulers of darkness and of this sort of air which is full of
powers. But if you have Christ, you will conquer this
entire world. That which you will open for yourself, you
will open. That which you will knock upon for yourself,
you will knock upon, benefiting yourself.

Help yourself, my son, by not proceeding with things
in which there is no profit.

My son, first purify yourself toward the outward life
in order that you may be able to purify the inward.

And be not as the merchants of the Word of God.

Put all words to the test first before you utter them.

Do not wish to acquire honors which are insecure, nor
the boastfulness which brings you to perdition.

Accept the wisdom of Christ who is patient and mild,
and guard this, O my son, knowing that God's way is
always profitable.

THE TEACHING OF SILVANUS

LOVE the truth, and the lie use like poison.

May the right time precede your words.

Speak when it is not proper to be silent, but speak
concerning the things you know . . . when it is fitting.

The untimely word is evidence of an evil mind.

When it is proper to act, do not use a word.

Do not wish to speak first in the midst of a crowd.

While it is a skill to speak, it is also a skill to be silent.

It is better for you to be defeated while speaking the truth, than to be victorious through deceit.

He who is victorious through deceit is defeated by the truth.

Untrue words are the evidence of evil persons.

Do not deceive anyone, especially him who needs advice.

If you speak after many others you will see more the advantage.

Wisdom leads the soul to the place of God.

There is no kinsman of the truth except wisdom.

It is not possible for a believing nature to become fond of lies.

A fearful and slavish nature will not be able to partake in faith.

When you are believing, what it is fitting to say is not more worthy than the hearing.

When you are with believing persons, desire to listen rather than to speak.

The sins of those who are ignorant are the shame of those who have taught them.

A wise man is a doer of good works after God.

May your life confirm your words before those who hear.

What it is not right to do, do not even consider doing.

What you do not want to happen to you, do not do yourself either.

He is a wise man who commends God to men, and God thinks more highly of the wise man than his own works.

After God, no one is as free as the wise man.

Everything God possesses the wise man has also.

Where your thought is, there is your goodness.

He who does not harm the soul neither does so to man.

After God, honor a wise man, since he is the servant of God.

To make the body of your soul a burden is pride, but to be able to restrain it gently when it is necessary is blessedness.

Someone who says, "I believe," even if he spends a long time pretending, he will not prevail, but he will fall; as your heart is, so will be your life.

A godly heart produces a blessed life.

Let not an ungrateful man cause you to cease to do good.

Persuade a senseless brother not to be senseless; if he is mad, protect him.

Strive eagerly to be victorious over every man in prudence; maintain self-sufficiency.

You cannot receive understanding except you know first that you possess nothing.

There is again this sentence. The members of the body are a burden to those who do not use them.

It is better to serve others than to make others serve you.

Not only do not hold an opinion which does not benefit the needy, but also do not listen to it.

He who gives something without respect commits an outrage.

If you take on the guardianship of orphans, you will be the father of many children since you are beloved of God.

He whom you serve because of honor, you have served for a wage.

If you give to him who will pay you respect . . . you have given not to man, but you gave for your own pleasure.

Speak concerning the word about God as if you were saying it in the presence of God.

If your mind is persuaded first that you have been god-loving, then speak to whomever you wish about God.

May your pious works precede every word about God.

It is better for you to be silent about the word of God than to speak recklessly.

It is not possible for you to know God when you do not worship him.

A man who does evil to someone will not be able to worship God.

The love of man is the beginning of godliness.

He who takes care of men while praying for all of them—this is the truth of God.

It is God's business to save whom he wants; it is the business of the god-loving man to beseech God to save everyone.

A man who is worthy of God, he is God among men, and he is the son of God.

It is better for man to be without anything than to have many things while not giving to the needy; so also you, if you pray to God, he will not give to you.

If you, from your whole heart, give your bread to the hungry, the gift is small, but the willingness is great with God.

He who thinks that no one is in the presence of God, he is not humble toward God.

He who makes his mind like unto God according to his power, he is the one who honors God greatly.

God does not need anything, but he rejoices over those who give to the needy.

The faithful do not speak many words, but their works are numerous.

It is a faithful person fond of learning who is the worker of the truth.

If you do not do evil to anyone, you will not be afraid of anyone.

The tyrant cannot take away prosperity.

What it is right to do, do it willingly.

What it is not right to do, don't do it in any way.

Promise everything rather than to say, "I am wise."

What you do well, say with your mind that it is God who does it.

Know who God is, and know who is the one who thinks in you; a good man is the good work of God.

THE SENTENCES OF SEXTUS

III. Out of Africa

THIRD-CENTURY MEDITATIONS

> It is the nature of reason to have promptings to the
> contemplation of virtue and vice.

ORIGEN

IN the third century, Christian ethics and theology developed most surely and found most eloquent expression on African soil, with towering figures such as Tertullian and Cyprian of Carthage, and Origen and Clement of Alexandria leading the way. These two cities may have been on the same continent, but between the Latin church of Carthage and the Greek church of Alexandria lay as vast a gulf as that between vigorous prose and sublime poetry. The theology of the former was highly pragmatic and institutional in emphasis, that of the latter was speculative, philosophical, and individualistic. Yet both shared a moral rigorism and a profound dedication to the teaching office, each of which is reflected in the meditations collected here.

Tertullian, perhaps the most combative of all early Christian theologians, wrote scores of tractates, some exposing heresy, others devoted to the development of moral purity, still others offering expositions of theological concepts central to Christianity. We include a brief example of each, all three of which testify to Tertullian's colorful use of language and indebtedness to the canons of Latin rhetoric. Saint Cyprian, bishop of Carthage, was as much a pastor as a theologian. Forced into exile by Roman persecutors, he ministered his flock by letter until he was martyred in 258. Cyprian's contemporary, Commodian, is little known, but his Instructions, exerpted here, are emblematic of one form of early Christian meditation, a collection of teachings each directed at a specific group within the Christian community.

In chapter five we include representative meditations from the exegetical and moral writings of three great teachers: Clement of Alexandria; Origen (Clement's successor as head of the catechetical school); and Origen's student, Gregory Thaumaturgus. Clement, who might best be described as an orthodox Gnostic, defines faith in terms of knowledge ("the purification of the leading faculty of the soul"). He suggests that when one who "partakes gnostically (or by means of knowledge) with this holy quality devotes himself to contemplation, communing in purity with the divine, he enters more nearly into the state of impassible identity, so as no longer to have science and possess knowledge, but to *be* science and knowledge." By this reading, meditation upon that which is holy transfigures the devout student of holiness into holiness itself. Clement's school (carried on by Origen and Gregory) thus elevated knowledge and reason to a status equal to, perhaps even interchangeable with, that of faith. Here, Meditation, which in this sense is reasoned contemplation, becomes not only an opportunity for edification but also a technique for salvation.

F O U R

The African Tradition:
Latin Meditations

AMID these reefs and inlets, amid these shallows and straits of idolatry, Faith, her sails filled by the Spirit of God, navigates; safe if cautious, secure if intently watchful. But to such as are washed overboard is a deep whence is no out-swimming; to such as are run aground is inextricable shipwreck; to such as are engulfed is a whirlpool, where there is no breathing—even in idolatry. All waves thereof whatsoever suffocate; every eddy thereof sucks down unto Hades. Let no one say, "Who will so safely foreguard himself? We shall have to go out of the world!" As if it were not as well worthwhile to go out, as to stand in the world as an idolater! Nothing can be easier than caution against idolatry, if the fear of it be our leading fear; any "necessity" whatever is too trifling compared to such a peril. The reason why the Holy Spirit did, when the apostles at that time were consulting, relax the bond and yoke for us, was that we might be free to devote ourselves to the shunning of idolatry. This shall be our Law, the more fully to be administered the more ready it is to hand; a Law peculiar to Christians, by means whereof we are recognized and examined by heathens. This Law must be set before such as approach unto the Faith, and inculcated on such as are entering it; that, in approaching, they may deliberate; observing it, may persevere; not observing it, may renounce their name. We will see to it, if, after the type of the Ark, there shall be in the Church raven, kite, dog, and serpent. At all events, an idolater is not found in the type of the Ark: no animal has been fashioned to represent an idolater. Let not that be in the Church which was not in the Ark.

TERTULLIAN, "ON IDOLATRY"

THERE is one soul and many tongues, one spirit and various sounds; every country has its own speech, but the subjects of speech are common to all. God is everywhere, and the goodness of God is everywhere; demons are everywhere, and the cursing of them is everywhere; the invocation of divine judgment is everywhere, death is everywhere, and the sense of death is everywhere, and all the world over is found the witness of the soul. There is not a soul of man that does not, from the light that is in itself, proclaim the very things we are not permitted to speak above our breath. Most justly, then, every soul is a culprit as well as a witness: in the measure that it testifies for truth, the guilt of error lies on it; and on the day of judgment it will stand before the courts of God, without a word to say. Thou proclaimedst God, O soul, but thou didst not seek to know him: evil spirits were detested by thee, and yet they were the objects of they adoration; the punishments of Hell were foreseen by thee, but no care was taken to avoid them; thou hadst a savor of Christianity, and withal wert the persecutor of Christians.

TERTULLIAN, "THE SOUL'S TESTAMENT"

SO amply sufficient a Depositary of patience is God. If it be a wrong which you deposit in his care, he is an Avenger; if a loss, he is a Restorer; if pain, he is a Healer; if death, he is a Reviver. What honor is granted to Patience, to have God as her Debtor! And not without reason: for she keeps all his decrees; she has to do with all his mandates. She fortifies faith; is the pilot of peace; assists charity; establishes humility; waits long for repentance; sets her seal on confession; rules the flesh; preserves the spirit; bridles the tongue; restrains the hand; tramples temptations under foot; drives away scandals; gives their crowning grace to martyrdoms; consoles the poor; teaches the rich moderation; overstrains not the weak; exhausts not the strong; is the delight of the believer; invites the Gentile; commends the servant to his lord, and his lord to God; adorns the woman; makes the man approved; is loved in childhood, praised in youth, looked up to in age; is beauteous in either sex, in every time of life.

TERTULLIAN, "OF PATIENCE"

YOU say that you are wealthy and rich, and you think that you should use those things which God has willed you to possess. Use them, certainly, but for the things of salvation; use them, but for good purposes; use them, but for those things which God has commanded, and which the Lord has set forth. Let the poor feel that you are wealthy; let the needy feel that you are rich. Lend your estate to God; give food to Christ. Move him by the prayers of many to grant you to carry out the glory of virginity, and to succeed in coming to the Lord's rewards. There entrust your treasures, where no thief digs through, where no

insidious plunderer breaks in. Prepare for yourself
possessions; but let them rather be heavenly ones, where
neither rust wears out, nor hail bruises, nor sun burns, nor
rain spoils your fruits constant and perennial, and free from
all contact of worldly injury. For in this very matter you
are sinning against God, if you think that riches were given
you by him for this purpose, to enjoy them thoroughly,
without a view to salvation. For God gave man also a
voice; and yet love songs and indecent things are not on
that account to be sung. And God willed iron to be for the
culture of the earth, but not on that account must murders
be committed. Or because God ordained incense and wine
and fire, are we thence to sacrifice to idols? Or because the
flocks of cattle abound in your fields, ought you to
immolate victims and offerings to the gods? Otherwise a
large estate is a temptation, unless the wealth minister to
good uses; so that every man, in proportion to his wealth,
ought by his patrimony rather to redeem his transgressions
than to increase them.

SAINT CYPRIAN, "TREATISE 2"

I

Thou seekest to wage war, O fool, as if wars were at
peace. From the first formed day in the end you fight. Lust
precipitates you, there is war; fight with it. Luxury
persuades, neglect it; thou hast overcome the war. Be
sparing of abundance of wine, lest by means of it thou
shouldest go wrong. Restrain thy tongue from cursing,
because with it thou adorest the Lord. Repress rage. Make
thyself peaceable to all. Beware of trampling on thy
inferiors when weighed down with miseries. Lend thyself
as a protector only, and do no hurt. Lead yourselves in a
righteous path, unstained by jealousy. In thy riches make

thyself gentle to those that are of little account. Give of
thy labor, clothe the naked. Thus shalt thou conquer. Lay
snares for no man, since thou servest God. Look to the
beginning, whence the envious enemy has perished. I am
not a teacher, but the law itself teaches by its proclamation.
Thou wearest such great words vainly, who in one moment
seekest without labor to raise a martyrdom to Christ.

II

In desiring, thence thou perishest, whilst thou art burning
with envy of thy neighbor. Thou extinguishest thyself,
when thou inflamest thyself within. Thou art jealous, O
envious man, of another who is struggling with evil, and
desirest that thou mayest become equally the possessor of
so much wealth. The law does not thus behold him when
thou seekest to fall upon him. Depending on all things,
thou livest in the lust of gain; and although thou art guilty
to thyself, thou condemnest thyself by thy own judgment.
The greedy survey of the eyes is never satisfied. Now,
therefore, if thou mayest return and consider, lust is vain
. . . whence God cries out, Thou fool, this night thou art
summoned. Death rushes after thee. Whose, then, shall be
those talents? By hiding the unrighteous gains in the
concealed treasury, when the Lord shall supply to everyone
his daily life. Let another accumulate; do thou seek to live
well. And when thy heart is conscious of God, thou shalt
be victor over all things; yet I do not say that thou
shouldest boast thyself in public, when thou art watching
for thy day by living without fraud. The bird perishes in
the midst of food, or carelessly sticks fast in the bird-lime.
Think that in thy simplicity thou hast much to beware of.
Let others transgress these bounds. Do thou always look
forward.

III

Why dost thou senselessly feign thyself good by the wound
of another? Whence thou bestowest, another is daily
weeping. Dost not thou believe that the Lord sees those
things from Heaven? The Highest says, he does not
approve of the gifts of the wicked. Thou shalt break forth
upon the wretched when thou shalt have gained a place.
One gives gifts that he may make another of no account; or
if thou hast lent on usury, taking twenty-four percent, thou
wishest to bestow charity that thou mayest purge thyself, as
being evil, with that which is evil. The Almighty absolutely
rejects such works as these. Thou hast given that which has
been wrung from tears; that candidate, oppressed with
ungrateful usuries, and become needy, deplores it. Besides
having obtained an opportunity for the exactors, thy enemy
for the present is the people; thou consecrated, hast become
wicked for reward. Also thou wishes to atone for thyself by
the gain of wages. O wicked one, thou deceivest thyself,
but none else.

IV

I warn certain readers only to consider, and to give material
to others by an example of life, to avoid strife, and to shun
so many quarrels; to repress terror, and never to
be proud; moreover, denounce the righteous obedience of
wicked men. Make yourselves like to Christ your Master,
O little ones. Be among the lilies of the field by your
benefits; ye have become blessed when ye bear the edicts;
ye are flowers in the congregation; ye are Christ's lanterns.
Keep what ye are, and ye shall be able to tell it.

V

Exercise the mystery of Christ, O deacons, with purity;
therefore, O ministers, do the commands of your Master;
do not play the person of a righteous judge; strengthen
your office by all things, as learned men, looking upward,
always devoted to the Supreme God. Render the faithful
sacred ministries of the altar to God, prepared in divine
matters to set an example; yourselves incline your head to
the pastors, so shall it come to pass that ye may be
approved of Christ.

VI

A shepherd, if he shall have confessed, has doubled his
conflict. Moreover, the apostle bids that such should be
teachers. Let him be a patient ruler; let him know when he
may relax the reins; let him terrify at first, and then anoint
with honey; and let him first observe to do himself what he
says. The shepherd who minds worldly things is esteemed
in fault, against whose countenance thou mightest dare to
say anything. Gehenna itself bubbles up in Hell with
rumors. Woe to the wretched people which wavers with
doubtful brow! If such a shepherd shall be present to it, it is
almost ruined. But a devout man restrains it, governing
rightly. The swarms are rejoiced under suitable kings; in
such there is hope, and the entire Church lives.

VII

If thy brother should be weak—I speak of the poor
man—do not empty-handed visit such a one as he lies ill.
Do good under God; pay your obedience by your money.

Thence he shall be restored; or if he should perish, let a poor man be refreshed, who has nothing wherewith to pay you, but the Founder and Author of the world on his behalf. Or if it should displease thee to go to the poor man, always hateful, send money, and something whence he may recover himself. And, similarly, if thy poor sister lies upon a sickbed, let your matrons begin to bear her victuals. God himself cries out, Break thy bread to the needy. There is no need to visit with words, but with benefits. It is wicked that thy brother should be sick through want of food. Satisfy him not with words. He needs meat and drink. Look upon such assuredly weakened, who are not able to act for themselves. Give to them at once. I pledge my word that fourfold shall be given you by God.

VIII

What can healthful poverty do, unless wealth be present? Assuredly, if thou hast the means, at once communicate also to thy brother. Be responsible to thyself for one, lest thou shouldst be said to be proud. I promise that thou shalt live more secure than the rich man. Receive into thy ears the teaching of the great Solomon: God hates the poor man to be a pleader on high. Therefore submit thyself, and give honor to him that is powerful; for the soft speech—thou knowest the proverb—melts. One is conquered by service, even although there be an ancient anger. If the tongue be silent, thou hast found nothing better. If there should not wholesomely be an art whereby life may be governed, either give aid or direction by the command of him that is mighty. Let it not shame or grieve you that a healthy man should have faith. In the treasury, besides, thou oughtest to give of thy labor, even as that widow whom the Anointed One preferred.

IX

Thou art luxurious with thy lips, with which thou oughtest
to groan. Shut up thy breast to evils, or loose them in thy
breast. But since the possession of money gives
barefacedness to the wealthy, thence everyone perishes
when they are most trusting to themselves. Thus,
moreover, the women assemble, as if they would enter the
bath. They press closely, and make of God's house as if it
were a fair. Certainly the Lord frightened the house of
prayer. The Lord's priest commanded with "sursum
corda," when prayer was to be made, that your silence
should be made. Thou answerest fluently, and moreover
abstainest not from promises. He entreats the Highest on
behalf of a devoted people, lest anyone should perish, and
thou turnest thyself to fables. Thou mockest at him, or
detractest from thy neighbor's reputation. Thou speakest in
an undisciplined manner, as if God were absent—as if he
who made all things neither hears nor sees.

X

I place no limit to a drunkard; but I prefer a beast. From
those who are proud in drinking thou withdrawest in thine
inner mind, holding the power of the ruler, O fool, among
Cyclopes. Thence in the histories thou criest, While I am
dead I drink not. Be it mine to drink the best things, and to
be wise in heart. Rather give assistance (what more seekest
thou to abuse?) to the lowest pauper, and ye shall both be
refreshed. If thou doest such things, thou extinguishest
Gehenna for thyself.

XI

Ye who are to be inhabitants of the heavens with
God-Christ, hold fast the beginning, look at all things from
Heaven. Let simplicity, let meekness dwell in your body.
Be not angry with thy devout brother without a cause, for
ye shall receive whatever ye may have done from him. This
has pleased Christ, that the dead should rise again, yea,
with their bodies; and those, too, whom in this world the
fire has burned, when six thousand years are completed,
and the world has come to an end. The Heaven in the
meantime is changed with an altered course, for then the
wicked are burnt up with divine fire. The creature with
groaning burns with the anger of the highest God. Those
who are more worthy, and who are begotten of an
illustrious stem, and the men of nobility under the
conquered Antichrist, according to God's command living
again in the world for a thousand years, indeed, that they
may serve the saints, and the High One, under a servile
yoke, that they may bear victuals on their neck. Moreover,
that they may be judged again when the reign is finished.
They who make God of no account when the thousandth
year is finished shall perish by fire, when they themselves
shall speak to the mountains. All flesh in the monuments
and tombs is restored according to its deed: they are
plunged in Hell; they bear their punishments in the world;
they are shown to them, and they read the things transacted
from Heaven; the reward according to one's deeds in a
perpetual tyranny.

THE INSTRUCTIONS OF COMMODIAN

FIVE

The Alexandrian School:
Greek Meditations

FAITH is a comprehensive knowledge of the essentials;
and knowledge is the strong and sure demonstration of
what is received by faith, built upon faith by the Lord's
teaching, conveying the soul on to infallibility, science, and
comprehension. And, in my view, the first saving change is
that from heathenism to faith . . . ; and the second, that
from faith to knowledge. And the latter terminating in
love, thereafter gives the loving to the loved, that which
knows to that which is known. And, perchance, such a one
has already attained the condition of "being equal to the
angels." Accordingly, after the highest excellence in the
flesh, changing always duly to the better, he urges his flight
to the ancestral hall, through the holy septenniad of
heavenly abodes to the Lord's own mansion; to be a light,
steady, and continuing eternally, entirely and in every part
immutable.

CLEMENT OF ALEXANDRIA,
"STROMATA"

HE called the "pure in heart blessed, for they shall see
God." And if we really look to the truth of the matter,
knowledge is the purification of the leading faculty of the

soul, and is a good activity. Some things accordingly are good in themselves, and others by participation in what is good, as we say good actions are good. But without things intermediate which hold the place of material, neither good nor bad actions are constituted, such I mean as life, and health, and other necessary things or circumstantials. Pure then as respects corporeal lusts, and pure in respect of holy thoughts, he means those are, who attain to the knowledge of God, when the chief faculty of the soul has nothing spurious to stand in the way of its power. When, therefore, he who partakes gnostically of this holy quality devotes himself to contemplation, communing in purity with the divine, he enters more nearly into the state of impassible identity, so as no longer to have science and possess knowledge, but to be science and knowledge.

CLEMENT OF ALEXANDRIA,
"STROMATA"

OUR holy Savior applied poverty and riches, and the like, both to spiritual things and objects of sense. For when he said, "Blessed are they that are persecuted for righteousness' sake," he clearly taught us in every circumstance to seek for the martyr who, if poor for righteousness' sake, witnesses that righteousness which he loves is a good thing; and if he "hunger and thirst for righteousness' sake," testifies that righteousness is the best thing. Likewise he, that weeps and mourns for righteousness' sake, testifies to the best law that it is beautiful. As, then, "those that are persecuted," so also "those that hunger and thirst" for righteousness' sake, are called "blessed" by him who approves of the true desire, which not even famine can put a stop to. And if "they hunger after righteousness itself," they are blessed. "And blessed are the poor," whether "in spirit" or in circumstances—that is, if for righteousness' sake. It is not the poor simply, but those that have wished to become poor for righteousness' sake, that he pronounces blessed—those who have despised the honors of this world in order to attain "the good"; likewise also those who, through chastity, have become comely in person and character, and those who are of noble birth, and honorable, having through righteousness attained to adoption, and therefore "have received power to become the sons of God," and "to tread on serpents and scorpions," and to rule over demons and "the host of the adversary." And, in fine, the Lord's discipline draws the soul away gladly from the body, even if it wrench itself away in its removal. "For he that loveth his life shall lose it, and he that loseth his life shall find it," if we only join that which is mortal of us with the immortality of God. It is the will of God that we should attain the knowledge of God, which is the communication of immortality. He therefore, who, in accordance with the word of repentence, knows his life to be sinful will lose it—losing it from sin, from which it is wrenched; but losing it, will find it, according to the obedience which lives again to faith, but dies to sin. This, then, is what it is "to find one's life," to know one's self.

CLEMENT OF ALEXANDRIA,
"STROMATA"

FIT objects for admiration are the Stoics, who say that the soul is not affected by the body, either to vice by disease, or to virtue by health; but both these things, they say, are indifferent. And indeed Job, through exceeding continence and excellence of faith, when from rich he became poor, from being held in honor dishonored, from being comely unsightly, and sick from being healthy, is depicted as a good example, putting the Tempter to shame, blessing his Creator; bearing what came second, as the first, and most clearly teaching that it is possible for the Gnostic to make an excellent use of all circumstances. And that ancient achievements are proposed as images for our correction, the apostle shows, when he says, "So that my bonds in Christ are become manifest in all the palace, and to all the rest; and several of the brethren in the Lord, waxing confident by my bonds, are much more bold to speak the word of God without fear"—since martyrs' testimonies are examples of conversion gloriously sanctified. For what things the Scripture speaks were written for our instruction, that we, through patience and the consolation of the Scriptures, might have the hope of consolation. When pain is present, the soul appears to decline from it, and to deem release from present pain a precious thing. At that moment it slackens from studies, when the other virtues also are neglected. And yet we do not say that it is virtue itself which suffers, for virtue is not affected by disease. But he who is partaker of both, of virtue and the disease, is afflicted by the pressure of the latter; and if he who has not yet attained the habit of self-command be not a high-souled man, he is distraught; and the inability to endure it is found equivalent to fleeing from it.

The same holds good also in the case of poverty. For it compels the soul to desist from necessary things, I mean contemplation and from pure sinlessness, forcing him, who has not wholly dedicated himself to God in love, to occupy himself about provisions; as, again, health and abundance of necessaries keep the soul free and unimpeded, and capable of making a good use of what is at hand. "For," says the apostle, "such shall have trouble in the flesh. But I spare you. For I would have you without anxiety, in order to decorum and assiduity for the Lord, without distraction."

These things, then, are to be abstained from, not for

their own sakes, but for the sake of the body; and care for the body is exercised for the sake of the soul, to which it has reference. For on this account it is necessary for the man who lives as a Gnostic to know what is suitable. Since the fact that pleasure is not a good thing is admitted from the fact that certain pleasures are evil, by this reason good appears evil, and evil good. And then, if we choose some pleasures and shun others, it is not every pleasure that is a good thing.

CLEMENT OF ALEXANDRIA, "STROMATA"

IF anyone spends his time on reading the Gospels, or the apostolic writings, and trains himself in the commandments of the New Testament, he, too, is rich, yet not rich, in all utterance, only in the Gospels and the apostolic books. But if he has power to learn by heart with equal diligence the New Testament and the Old, and to be so instructed by all their learning that he is ready to explain particular points in the Scriptures, and to regulate his life according to the word of truth contained in the Scriptures—he indeed is rich in all utterance and in every good work. I believe it is of these riches that it is said, the ransom of a man's life is his riches. Better then the little thing the righteous hath than the great riches of the wicked.

ORIGEN, "HOMILIES ON THE PSALMS"

THE rational creature in addition to its fantastic nature has reason, which distinguishes between the fantasies, rejecting some, approving others, so that the creature may be guided accordingly. Now it is the nature of reason to have promptings to the contemplation of virtue and vice; and if, yielding to these promptings, we choose the former ourselves and shun the latter, we deserve praise for devoting ourselves to the practice of virtue, or blame if we take the opposite course. We must not, however, fail to remark that, though for the most part the nature of animals is adapted to all their needs, it is so in varying degrees, sometimes more, sometimes less; so that hounds in hunting and horses in war are not, if I may say so, far from the rational creature. Now, whether something external shall chance to excite this or that fantasy in us, confessedly does not rest with us; but it is for reason and nothing else to decide whether we shall use what has happened in a particular way or otherwise, reason either urging us, according to its promptings to follow our better and nobler instincts, or misleading us so that we do the reverse.

If anyone says that the outward world is so constituted that one cannot resist it, let him study his own feelings and movements, and see whether there are not some plausible motives to account for his approval and assent, and the inclination of his reason to a particular object.

ORIGEN, "THE PHILOKALIA"

NOW he is called the light of men and the true light and the light of the world, because he brightens and irradiates the higher parts of men or, in a word, of all reasonable beings. And similarly it is from and because of the energy with which he causes the old deadness to be put aside and that which is *par excellence* life to be put on so that those who have truly received him rise again from the dead, that he is called the resurrection. And this he does not only at the moment at which a man says, "We are buried with Christ through baptism and have risen again with him," but much rather when a man, having laid off all about him that belongs to death, walks in the newness of life which belongs to him, the Son, while here. We always "carry about in our body the dying of the Lord Jesus," and thus we reap the vast advantage, "that the life of the Lord Jesus might be made manifest in our bodies."

But that progress, too, which is in wisdom and which is found by those who seek their salvation in it to do for them what they require both in respect of exposition of truth in the divine word and in respect of conduct according to true righteousness, it lets us understand how Christ is the way. In this way we have to take nothing with us, neither wallet nor coat; we must travel without even a stick, nor must we have shoes on our feet. For this road is itself sufficient for all the supplies of our journey; and everyone who walks on it wants nothing. He is clad with a garment which is fit for one who is setting out in response to an invitation to a wedding; and on this road he cannot meet anything that can annoy him. "No one," Solomon says, "can find out the way of a serpent upon a rock." I would add, or that of any other beast. Hence there is no need of a staff on this road, on which there is no trace of any hostile creature, and the hardness of which, whence also it is called rock, makes it incapable of harboring anything hurtful.

Further, the Only-begotten is the truth, because he embraces in himself according to the Father's will the whole reason of all things, and that with perfect clearness, and being the truth communicates to each creature in proportion to its worthiness. And should anyone inquire whether all that the Father knows, according to the depth of his riches and his wisdom and his knowledge, is known to our Savior also, and should he, imagining that he will thereby glorify the Father, show that some things known to the Father are unknown to the Son, although he might have had an equal share of the apprehensions of the unbegotten God, we must remind him that it is from his being the truth that he is Savior, and add that if he is the truth complete, then there is nothing true which he does not know; truth must not limp for the want of the things which, according to those persons, are known to the Father only. Or else let it be shown that some things are known to which the name of truth does not apply, but which are above the truth.

It is clear also that the principle of that life which is pure and unmixed with any other element resides in him who is the firstborn of all creation, taking from which those who have a share in Christ live the life which is true life, while all those who are thought to live apart from this, as they have not the true light, have not the true life either.

ORIGEN, "COMMENTARY ON JOHN"

THE single eye is the love unfeigned; for when the body is enlightened by it, it sets forth through the medium of the outer members only things which are perfectly correspondent with the inner thoughts. But the evil eye is the pretended love, which is also called hypocrisy, by which the whole body of the man is made darkness. We have to consider that deeds meet only for darkness may be within the man, while through the outer members he may produce words that seem to be of the light; for there are those who are in reality wolves, though they may be covered with sheep's clothing. Such are they who wash only the outside of the cup and platter, and do not understand that, unless the inside of these things is cleansed, the outside itself cannot be made pure. Wherefore, in manifest confutation of such persons, the Savior says: "If the light that is in thee be darkness, how great is that darkness!" That is to say, if the love which seems to thee to be light is really a work meet for darkness, by reason of some hypocrisy concealed in thee, what must be thy patent transgressions!

GREGORY THAUMATURGUS,
"ON THE GOSPEL OF SAINT MATTHEW"

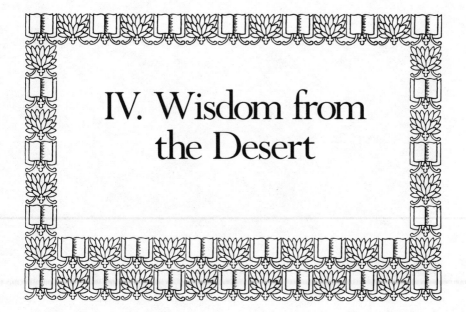

IV. Wisdom from the Desert

> The contemplation of God is gained in a
> variety of ways.
>
> JOHN CASSIAN

I F one were to attempt a more precise definition of early
Christian "meditations" than we have chosen for this inclu-
sive collection of devotions, one group of writings would
surely emerge as emblematic of the genre: the wisdom from
the desert. Three primary examples of this wisdom, each distin-
guished by profound spiritual conviction and a special commitment
to the teaching office, are excerpted here. Each is a collection of
sayings. One parallel (though far from the desert sayings) is the
Jewish Sayings of the Fathers, or *Pirke Aboth,* wise thoughts and
evocative stories of holy teachers compiled during the late first and
early second centuries and collected in a special section of the
Mishna.

Here we offer three different collections of sayings, each
distinctive. Writing in Greek, Evagrius Ponticus, a student of the
Alexandrian school, offers a kind of philosophical asceticism; the
Latin-speaking John Cassian, though influenced by Evagrius, ex-
emplifies in the wisdom of the desert fathers a somewhat more
practical asceticism; and the Sayings of the Fathers themselves, cast
in the form of simple stories, exemplify what might be called
unadorned asceticism.

Evagrius Ponticus lived in the late fourth century, was ordained by Saint Gregory of Nazianzus, and began his religious
career as a preacher in Constantinople. At the age of thirty-six, he
left the city for the desert. Claiming that "the virtues have
knowledge for their fruit," he was condemned by people who
discerned in his writings certain of Origen's "heretical" tendencies.
But even as Origen is widely accepted today as a preeminent early
Christian teacher, Evagrius Ponticus bridges the centuries with his
philosophical profession of monastic faith. We include selections of
his *Praktikos,* a series of meditations on the principle of *apatheia,* or
freedom from passion and desire, which, like other of the Alexandrian teachings, has a decidedly Oriental theological cast.

Chapter seven is devoted to a selection from John Cassian's

voluminous conferences or dialogues, with leading abbots in various Eastern monasteries. They were collected for the instruction and edification of monks and Christian lay people in the West. Cassian, who lived in the late fourth and early fifth centuries, founded two monasteries near Marseilles, where the *Conferences* were written.

This section closes with excerpts from the *Sayings of the Desert Fathers,* a compendium of wisdom from Egyptian monks of the third and fourth centuries. Unlike Cassian's dialogues, these meditations are cast in the form of parables, or stories from life, each illuminating in some simple yet poignant way the essence of faith and faithfulness.

SIX

The Praktikos of Evagrius Ponticus

I

CHRISTIANITY is the dogma of Christ our Savior. It is composed of *praktike,* of the contemplation of the physical world and of the contemplation of God.

II

The kingdom of Heaven is *apatheia* of the soul along with true knowledge of existing things.

III

Whatever a man loves he will desire with all his might. What he desires he strives to lay hold of. Now desire precedes every pleasure, and it is feeling which gives birth to desire. For that which is not subject to feeling is also free of passion.

IV

The thought of gluttony suggests to the monk that he give up his ascetic efforts in short order. It brings to his mind concern for his stomach, for his liver and spleen, the thought of a long illness, scarcity of the commodities of life, and finally of his edematous body and the lack of care by the physicians. These things are depicted vividly before his eyes. It frequently brings him to recall certain ones among the brethren who have fallen upon such sufferings. There even comes a time when it persuades those who suffer from such maladies to visit those who are practicing a life of abstinence and to expose their misfortune and relate how these came about as a result of the ascetic life.

V

The demon of impurity impels one to lust after bodies. It attacks more strenuously those who practice continence, in the hope that they will give up their practice of this virtue, feeling that they gain nothing by it. This demon has a way of bowing the soul down to practices of an impure kind, defiling it, and causing it to speak and hear certain words almost as if the reality were actually present to be seen.

VI

Avarice suggests to the mind a lengthy old age, inability to perform manual labor (at some future date), famines that are sure to come, sickness that will visit us, the pinch of poverty, the great shame that comes from accepting the necessities of life from others.

VII

Sadness tends to come up at times because of the deprivations of one's desires. On other occasions it accompanies anger. When it arises from the deprivation of desires, it takes place in the following manner. Certain thoughts first drive the soul to the memory of home and parents, or else to that of one's former life. Now when these thoughts find that the soul offers no resistance but rather follows after them and pours itself out in pleasures that are still only mental in nature, they then seize her and drench her in sadness, with the result that these ideas she was just indulging no longer remain. In fact, they cannot be had in reality, either, because of her present way of life. So the miserable soul is now shriveled up in her humiliation to the degree that she poured herself out upon these thoughts of hers.

VIII

The most fierce passion is anger. In fact, it is defined as a boiling and stirring up of wrath against one who has given injury—or is thought to have done so. It constantly irritates the soul and above all at the time of prayer it seizes the mind and flashes the picture of the offensive person before one's eyes. Then there comes a time when it persists longer, is transformed into indignation, stirs up alarming experiences by night. This is succeeded by a general debility of the body, malnutrition with its attendant pallor, and the illusion of being attacked by poisonous wild beasts. These four last mentioned consequences following upon indignation may be found to accompany many thoughts.

IX

The demon of *acedia*—also called the noonday demon—is the one that causes the most serious trouble of all. He presses his attack upon the monk about the fourth hour and besieges the soul until the eighth hour. First of all, he

makes it seem that the sun barely moves, if at all, and that
the day is fifty hours long. Then he constrains the monk to
look constantly out the windows, to walk outside the cell,
to gaze carefully at the sun to determine how far it stands
from the ninth hour, to look now this way and now that to
see if perhaps one of the brethren appears from his cell.
Then, too, he instills in the heart of the monk a hatred for
the place, a hatred for his very life itself, a hatred for
manual labor. He leads him to reflect that charity has
departed from among the brethren, that there is no one to
give encouragement. Should there be someone at this
period who happens to offend him in some way or other,
this, too, the demon uses to contribute further to his
hatred. This demon drives him along to desire other sites
where he can more easily procure life's necessities, more
readily find work and make a real success of himself. He
goes on to suggest that, after all, it is not the place that is
the basis of pleasing the Lord. God is to be adored
everywhere. He joins to these reflections the memory of his
dear ones and of his former way of life. He depicts life
stretching out for a long period of time, and brings before
the mind's eye the toil of the ascetic struggle and, as the
saying has it, leaves no leaf unturned to induce the monk to
forsake his cell and drop out of the fight. No other demon
follows close upon the heels of this one (when he is
defeated) but only a state of deep peace and inexpressible
joy arise out of this struggle.

X

The spirit of vainglory is most subtle, and it readily grows
up in the souls of those who practice virtue. It leads them
to desire to make their struggles known publicly, to hunt
after the praise of men.

XI

The man who flees from all worldly pleasures is an impregnable tower before the assaults of the demon of sadness. For sadness is a deprivation of sensible pleasure, whether actually present or only hoped for. And so if we continue to cherish some affection for anything in this world, it is impossible to repel this enemy, for he lays his snares and produces sadness precisely where he sees we are particularly inclined.

XII

Both anger and hatred increase anger. But almsgiving and meekness diminish it even when it is present.

XIII

Let not the sun go down upon our anger lest by night the demons come upon us to strike fear in our souls and render our spirits more cowardly for the fight on the morrow. For images of a frightful kind usually arise from anger's disturbing influence. Indeed, there is nothing more disposed to render the spirit inclined to desertion than troubled irascibility.

XIV

Be very attentive lest ever you cause some brother to become a fugitive through your anger. For if this should happen your whole life long you will yourself not be able to flee from the demon of sadness. At the time of prayer this will be a constant stumbling block to you.

XV

A gift snuffs out the fire of resentment, as Jacob well knew. For he flattered Esau with gifts when he went out to meet him with four hundred men. But as for ourselves who are poor men we must supply for our lack of gifts by the table we lay.

XVI

It is only with considerable difficulty that one can escape the thought of vainglory. For what you do to destroy it becomes the principle of some other form of vainglory. Now the demons do not oppose every good thought of ours, the vices which we have also oppose some of them.

XVII

I have observed the demon of vainglory being chased by nearly all the other demons, and when his pursuers fell, shamelessly he drew near and unfolded a long list of his virtues.

XVIII

The demons that rule over the passions of the soul persevere until death. Those which rule over the bodily passions depart more quickly. . . .

XIX

The passions are accustomed to be stirred up by the senses, so that when charity and continence are lodged in the soul, then the passions are not stirred up. And when they are absent, the passions are stirred up. Anger stands more in need of remedies than concupiscence, and for that reason the love that is charity is to be reckoned a great thing indeed in that it is able to bridle anger. The great and holy man Moses, where he treats of the things of nature, refers to it symbolically as the killer of snakes.

XX

Those who give but scant nourishment to their bodies and yet "take thought for the flesh to satisfy its lusts" have only themselves to blame and not their bodies. For those who have attained to purity of heart by means of the body and who in some measure have applied themselves to the contemplation of created things know the grace of the Creator in giving them a body.

XXI

Natural processes which occur in sleep without accompanying images of a stimulating nature are, to a certain measure, indications of a healthy soul. But images that are distinctly formed are a clear indication of sickness. You may be certain that the faces one sees in dreams are, when they occur as ill-defined images, symbols of former affective experiences. Those which are seen clearly, on the other hand, indicate wounds that are still fresh.

XXII

We recognize the indications of *apatheia* by our thoughts
during the day, but we recognize it by our dreams during
the night. We call *apatheia* the health of the soul. The food
of the soul can be said to be contemplative knowledge since
it alone is able to unite us with the holy powers.

XXIII

The demon of vainglory lives in a state of opposition to
the demon of impurity, so that it is not possible for both
of them to assault the soul at the same time. For the one
promises honors while the other becomes the agent of
dishonor. And so whichever of these two draws near to
harass you, feign that the thoughts of the other antagonist
is present within you. Should you then be able, as the
saying has it, to drive out a nail with a nail, you can know
for certain that you stand near the confines of *apatheia,* for
your mind is strong enough to abolish thoughts inspired by
the demons with human thoughts. Beyond any doubt, the
ability to drive away the thought of vainglory through
humility, or the power to repel the demon of impurity
through temperance, is a most profound proof of *apatheia.*
Make every attempt to deal in this same way with all the
demons that are mutually opposed to one another. At the
same time, learn to recognize by which emotion you are
more inclined to be led astray, and employ your whole
strength in pleading with God to ward off your enemies in
this second manner also.

XXIV

Both the virtues and the vices make the mind blind. The one so that it may not see the vices; the other, in turn, so that it might not see the virtues.

XXV

The proof of *apatheia* is had when the spirit begins to see its own light, when it remains in a state of tranquility in the presence of the images it has during sleep, and when it maintains its calm as it beholds the affairs of life.

XXVI

The soul which has *apatheia* is not simply the one which is not disturbed by changing events but the one which remains unmoved at the memory of them as well.

XXVII

The perfect man does not work at remaining continent, nor does the man with *apatheia* work at being patient. For patience is the virtue of a man who experiences untoward emotions and continence is the virtue of a man who suffers disturbing impulses.

XXVIII

A man who has established the virtues in himself and is entirely permeated with them no longer remembers the law or commandments or punishment. Rather, he says and does what excellent habit suggests.

XXIX

The effects of keeping the commandments do not suffice to heal the powers of the soul completely. They must be complemented by a contemplative activity appropriate to these faculties, and this activity must penetrate the spirit.

XXX

The spirit that is engaged in the war against the passions does not see clearly the basic meaning of the war for it is something like a man fighting in the darkness of night. Once it has attained to purity of heart, though, it distinctly makes out the designs of the enemy.

XXXI

The rational soul operates according to nature when the following conditions are realized: the concupiscible part desires virtue; the irascible part fights to obtain it; the rational part, finally, applies itself to the contemplation of created things.

XXXII

The man who is progressing in the ascetic life diminishes the force of passion. The man progressing in contemplation diminishes his ignorance. As regards the passions, the time will come when they will be entirely destroyed. In the matter of ignorance, however, one type will have an end, but another type will not.

XXXIII

Those things which are good or evil according as they are used well or ill are the objects making up virtue or vice. Prudence is the virtue that employs these objects for the one or the other.

XXXIV

According to our master, that man of wisdom, the rational soul is composed of three parts. When virtue comes to birth in the rational part, it is called prudence, understanding, and wisdom. When it is developed in the concupiscible part, it receives the names of temperance, charity, and continence. Justice, however, is located in the whole of the soul. The virtue of the irascible part is termed courage and patience. Now the proper work of prudence is to war against the hostile powers and to protect the virtues, to draw up its forces against the vices, and to arrange affairs according to the requirements of the times. The province of understanding is to direct all those things which lead to our perfection in such a way that they harmoniously achieve their aim. Wisdom governs the contemplation of the meaningful structure of both corporeal and incorporeal objects. Temperance has the function of enabling us to look upon those affairs which cause irrational fantasms, remaining the while free of passion. Charity has the role of showing itself to every image of God as being as nearly like its prototype as possible no matter how the demons ply their arts to defile them. Continence has the power of refusing with joy every pleasure of the palate. The work of courage and patience is to know no fear of enemies and eagerly to endure afflictions. Finally, justice produces a certain harmony and symphony among the various parts of the soul.

XXXV

The sheaves of grain are the fruit of seeds; the virtues have knowledge as their fruit. As surely as tears go with the labor of sowing, joy attends the reaping.

SEVEN

John Cassian's
Conferences

THE contemplation of God is gained in a variety of ways.
For we not only discover God by admiring his
incomprehensible essence, a thing which still lies hid in the
hope of the promise, but we see him through the greatness
of his creation, and the consideration of his justice, and the
aid of his daily providence: when with pure minds we
contemplate what he has done with his saints in every
generation, when with trembling heart we admire his
power with which he governs, directs, and rules all things,
or the vastness of his knowledge, and that eye of his from
which no secrets of the heart can lie hid, when we consider
the sand of the sea, and the number of the waves measured
by him and known to him, when in our wonder we think
that the drops of rain, the days and hours of the ages, and
all things past and future are present to his knowledge;
when we gaze in unbounded admiration on that ineffable
mercy of his, which with unwearied patience endures
countless sins which are every moment being committed
under his very eyes, or the call with which from no
antecedent merits of ours, but by the free grace of his pity
he receives us; or again the numberless opportunities of
salvation which he grants to those whom he is going to
adopt—that he made us be born in such a way as that from
our very cradles his grace and the knowledge of his law

might be given to us, that he himself, overcoming our
enemy in us simply for the pleasure of his goodwill,
rewards us with eternal bliss and everlasting rewards, when
lastly he undertook the dispensation of his Incarnation for
our salvation, and extended the marvels of his sacraments
to all nations. But there are numberless other considerations
of this sort, which arise in our minds according to the
character of our life and the purity of our heart, by which
God is either seen by pure eyes or embraced, which
considerations certainly no one will preserve lastingly, if
anything of carnal affections still survives in him.

FIRST CONFERENCE OF ABBOT MOSES

RICHES and possessions are taken in holy Scripture in
three different ways, i.e., as good, bad, and indifferent.
Those are bad of which it is said: "The rich have wanted
and have suffered hunger," and "Woe unto you that are
rich, for ye have received your consolation": and to have
cast off these riches is the height of perfection; and a
distinction which belongs to those poor who are
commended in the gospel by the Lord's saying: "Blessed
are the poor in spirit, for theirs is the kingdom of Heaven";
and in the Psalm: "This poor man cried, and the Lord
heard him," and again: "The poor and needy shall praise
thy name." Those riches are good, to acquire which is the
work of great virtue and merit, and the righteous possessor
of which is praised by David who says, "The generation of
the righteous shall be blessed: glory and riches are in his
house, and his righteousness remaineth forever" and again
"the ransom of a man's life are his riches." . . . There are
some also which are indifferent, i.e., which may be made
either good or bad: for they are made either one or the
other in accordance with the will and character of those

who use them, of which the blessed Apostle says, "Charge
the rich of this world not to be high-minded nor to trust in
the uncertainty of riches, but in God (who giveth us
abundantly all things to enjoy), to do good, to give easily,
to communicate to others, to lay up in store for themselves
a good foundation that they may lay hold on the true life."
These are what the rich man in the gospel kept, and never
distributed to the poor—while the beggar Lazarus was
lying at his gate and desiring to be fed with his crumbs; and
so he was condemned to the unbearable flames and
everlasting heat of hell fire.

CONFERENCE OF ABBOT PAPHNUTIUS

THE mind of the upright man ought not to be like wax or
any other soft material which always yields to the shape of
what presses on it, and is stamped with its form and
impress and keeps it until it takes another shape by having
another seal stamped upon it; and so it results that it never
retains its own form but is turned and twisted about to
correspond to whatever is pressed upon it. But he should
rather be like some stamp of hard steel, that the mind may
always keep its proper form and shape inviolate, and may
stamp and imprint on everything which occurs to it the
marks of its own condition, while upon it itself nothing
that happens can leave any mark.

CONFERENCE OF ABBOT THEODORE

THE time spent here, and the dwelling in solitude, and
meditation, through which you think that we ought to have
attained perfection of the inner man, has only done this for

us; namely, teach us that which we are unable to be,
without making us what we are trying to be. Nor do we
feel that by this knowledge we have acquired any fixed
steadfastness of the purity which we long for, or any
strength and firmness; but only an increase of confusion and
shame: for though our meditation in all our discipline aims
at this in our dialy studies, and endeavors from trembling
beginnings to reach a sure and unwavering skill, and to
begin to know something of what originally it knew but
vaguely or was altogether ignorant of, and by advancing by
sure steps, so to speak, toward the condition of that
discipline, to habituate itself perfectly to it without any
difficulty, I find on the contrary that while I am struggling
in this desire for purity, I have only got far enough to
know what I cannot be. And hence I feel that nothing but
trouble results to me from all this contrition of heart, so
that matter for tears is never wanting, and yet I do not
cease to be what I ought not to be. And so what is the
good of having learnt what is best, if it cannot be attained
even when known? For when we have been feeling that the
aim of our heart was directed toward what we purposed,
insensibly the mind returns to its previous wandering
thoughts and slips back with a more violent rush, and is
taken up with daily distractions and incessantly drawn away
by numberless things that take it captive, so that we almost
despair of the improvement which we long for, and all
these observances seem useless. Since the mind which every
moment wanders off vaguely, when it is brought back to
the fear of God or spiritual contemplation, before it is
established in it, darts off and strays; and when we have
been roused and have discovered that it has wandered from
the purpose set before it, and want to recall it to the
meditation from which it has strayed, and to bind it fast
with the firmest purpose of heart, as if with chains, while
we are making the attempt it slips away from the inmost
recesses of the heart swifter than a snake. Wherefore we
being inflamed by daily exercises of this kind, and yet not

seeing that we gain from them any strength and stability in heart are overcome and in despair driven to this opinion; namely, to believe that it is from no fault of our own but from a fault of our nature that these wanderings of mind are found in mankind.

FIRST CONFERENCE OF ABBOT SERENUS

THE nature of the soul is not inaptly compared to a very fine feather or very light wing, which, if it has not been damaged or affected by being spoilt by any moisture falling on it from without, is borne aloft almost naturally to the heights of Heaven by the lightness of its nature, and the aid of the slightest breath; but if it is weighted by any moisture falling upon it and penetrating into it, it will not only not be carried away by its natural lightness into any aerial flights but will actually be borne down to the depths of earth by the weight of the moisture it has received. So also our soul, if it is not weighted with faults that touch it, and the cares of this world, or damaged by the moisture of injurious lusts, will be raised as it were by the natural blessing of its own purity and borne aloft to the heights by the light breath of spiritual meditation; and leaving things low and earthly will be transported to those that are heavenly and invisible. Wherefore we are well warned by the Lord's command: "Take heed that your hearts be not weighed down by surfeiting and drunkenness and the cares of this world." And therefore if we want our prayers to reach not only the sky but what is beyond the sky, let us be careful to reduce our soul, purged from all earthly faults and purified from every stain, to its natural lightness, that so our prayer may rise to God unchecked by the weight of any sin.

FIRST CONFERENCE OF ABBOT ISAAC

THERE is a great difference between one who puts out the fire of sin within him by fear of Hell or hope of future reward, and one who from the feeling of divine love has a horror of sin itself and of uncleanness, and keeps hold of the virtue of purity simply from the love and longing for purity, and looks for no reward from a promise for the future, but, delighted with the knowledge of good things present, does everything not from regard to punishment but from delight in virtue. For this condition can neither abuse an opportunity to sin when all human witnesses are absent, nor be corrupted by the secret allurements of thoughts, while, keeping in its very marrow the love of virtue itself, it not only does not admit into the heart anything that is opposed to it, but actually hates it with the utmost horror. For it is one thing for a man in his delight at some present good to hate the stains of sins and of the flesh, and another thing to check unlawful desires by contemplating the future reward; and it is one thing to fear present loss and another to dread future punishment. Lastly, it is a much greater thing to be unwilling to forsake good for good's own sake than it is to withhold consent from evil for fear of evil. For in the former case the good is voluntary, but in the latter it is constrained and as it were violently forced out of a reluctant party either by fear of punishment or by greed of reward. For one who abstains from the allurements of sin owing to fear will, whenever the obstacle of fear is removed, once more return to what he loves and thus will not continually acquire any stability in good, nor will he ever rest free from attacks because he will not secure the sure and lasting peace of chastity. For where there is the disturbance of warfare there cannot help being the danger of wounds. For one who is in the midst of the conflict, even though he is a warrior and by fighting bravely inflicts frequent and deadly wounds on his foes, must still sometimes be pierced by the point of the enemy's sword. But one who has defeated the attack of sins and is now in the enjoyment of the security of peace, and has passed on to the love of virtue itself, will keep this condition of good continually, as he is entirely wrapped up in it, because he believes that nothing can be worse than the loss of his inmost chastity. For he deems nothing dearer or more precious than present purity, to whom a dangerous departure from virtue or a poisonous stain of sin is a grievous punishment. To such a one, I say, neither will regard for the presence of another add anything to his goodness nor will solitude take anything away from it; but as always and everywhere he bears about with him his conscience as a judge not only of his actions but also of his thoughts, he will especially try to please it, as he knows that it cannot be cheated nor deceived, and that he cannot escape it.

FIRST CONFERENCE OF ABBOT CHAEREMON

IF you are anxious to attain to the light of spiritual knowledge, not wrongly for an idle boast but for the sake of being made better men, you are first inflamed with the longing for that blessedness, of which we read: "Blessed are the pure in heart for they shall see God," that you may also attain to that of which the angel said to Daniel: "But they that are learned shall shine as the splendor of the firmament: and they that turn many to rightousness as the stars forever and ever"; and in another prophet: "Enlighten yourselves with the light of knowledge while there is time." And so keeping up that diligence in reading, which I see that you have, endeavor with all eagerness to gain in the first place a thorough grasp of practical, i.e., ethical knowledge. For without this that theoretical purity of which we have spoken cannot be obtained, which those only, who are perfected not by the words of others who teach them, but by the excellence of their own actions, can after much expenditure of effort and toil attain as a reward for it. For as they gain their knowledge not from meditation on the law but from the fruit of their labor, they sing with the Psalmist: "From thy commandments I have understanding"; and having overcome all their passions, they say with confidence: "I will sing, and I will understand in the undefiled way." For he who is striving in an undefiled way in the course of a pure heart, as he sings the Psalm, understands the words which are chanted. . . . For it is one thing to have a ready tongue and elegant language, and quite another to penetrate into the very heart and marrow of heavenly utterances and to gaze with pure eye of the soul on profound and hidden mysteries; for this can be gained by no learning of man's, nor condition of this world, only by purity of soul, by means of the illumination of the Holy Ghost.

FIRST CONFERENCE OF ABBOT NESTEROS

IT is said that the blessed John, while he was gently stroking a partridge with his hands, suddenly saw a philosopher approaching him in the garb of a hunter, who was astonished that a man of so great fame and reputation should demean himself to such paltry and trivial amusements, and said: "Can you be that John, whose great and famous reputation attracted me also with the greatest desire for your acquaintance? Why then do you occupy yourself with such poor amusements?" To whom the blessed John: "What is it," said he, "that you are carrying in your hand?" The other replied: "A bow." "And why," said he, "do you not always carry it everywhere bent?" To whom the other replied: "It would not do, for the force of its stiffness would be relaxed by its being continually bent, and it would be lessened and destroyed, and when the time came for it to send stouter arrows after the beast, its stiffness would be lost by the excessive and continuous strain, and it would be impossible for the more powerful bolts to be shot." "And, my lad," said the blessed John, "do not let this slight and short relaxation of my mind disturb you, as unless it sometimes relieved and relaxed the rigor of its purpose by some recreation, the spirit would lose its spring owing to the unbroken strain and would be unable when need required implicitly to follow what was right."

CONFERENCE OF ABBOT ABRAHAM

E I G H T

Sayings of the
Desert Fathers

I

THE abbot Moses, who dwelt in Petra, was at one time sorely harried by lust; and when he could no longer endure to hold himself in his cell, he set out to tell it to the abbot Isidore, and the old man asked him to go back again to his cell. But he did not consent, saying, "I cannot, Father." And he took him and brought him into the house. And he said to him, "Look at the sunset." And he looked and saw a multitude of demons, and they were in commotion and rousing themselves to battle. And again the abbot Isidore said, "Look to the East." And he looked and saw an innumerable multitude of angels in glory. Whereupon the abbot Isidore said, "Behold, these are they that are sent to aid; those that are climbing up in the west are they that fight against us; and they that are with us are more than they that be against us." And the abbot Moses thanked God and took courage, and returned to his cell.

II

At one time Zachary went to his abbot Silvanus and found him in an ecstasy, and his hands were stretched out to Heaven. And when he saw him thus, he closed the door and went away; and coming back about the sixth hour and

the ninth, he found him even so; but toward the tenth hour
he knocked and, coming in, found him lying quiet and said
to him, "What ailed thee today, Father?" And he said, "I
was ill today, my son." But the young man held his feet,
saying, "I shall not let thee go until thou tell me what thou
hast seen." The old man answered him: "I was caught up
into Heaven, and I saw the glory of God. And I stood there
until now, and now am I sent away."

III

Said the abbot Antony: "I do not now fear God, but I love
him, for love casteth fear out of doors."

Again he said that with our neighbor there is life and
death; for if we do good to our brother, we shall do good
to God, but if we scandalize our brother, we sin against
Christ.

IV

At one time the abbot John was climbing up from Scete
with other brethren, and he who was by way of guiding
them mistook the way, for it was night. And the brethren
said to the abbot John, "What shall we do, Father, for the
brother has missed the way, and we may lose ourselves and
die?" And the old man said, "If we say aught to him, he
will be cast down. But I shall make a show of being worn
out and say that I cannot walk, but must lie here till
morning." And he did so. And the others said, "Neither
shall we go on but shall sit down beside thee." And they
sat down until morning, so as not to discountenance their
brother.

V

A brother asked a certain old man, saying, "There be two brothers, and one of them is quiet in his cell and prolongs his fast for six days and lays much travail on himself, but the other tends the sick. Whose work is the more acceptable to God?" And the old man answered, "If that brother who carries his fast for six days were to hang himself up by the nostrils, he could not equal the other, who does service to the sick."

VI

A certain brother asked an old man, saying, "Tell me, Father, wherefore is it that the monks travail in discipline and yet receive not such grace as the ancient Fathers had?" And the old man said to him, "Then was love so great that each man set his neighbor on high, but now hath love grown cold and the whole world is set in malice, and each doth pull down his neighbor to the lower room, and for this reason we come short of grace."

VII

The abbot Pambo asked the abbot Antony, saying, "What shall I do?" And the old man made answer, "Be not confident of thine own righteousness; grieve not over a thing that is past; and be continent of thy tongue and of thy belly."

VIII

A brother asked an old man, "How cometh the fear of God in a man?" And the old man said, "If a man have humility and poverty and judgeth not another, so comes in him the fear of God."

IX

The abbot Antony said, "Who sits in solitude and is quiet hath escaped from three wars: hearing, speaking, seeing; yet against one thing shall he continually battle: that is, his own heart."

X

The abbot Nilus said, "Invulnerable from the arrows of the enemy is he who loves quiet; but he who mixeth with the crowd hath often wounds."

XI

Certain brethren, being minded to go from Scete to the abbot Antony, went aboard a ship that they might go to him, and they found in that same ship an old man who likewise was minded to go to Antony. But the brethren did not know him. And as they sat in the ship they talked with one another about the sayings of the Fathers and about the Scriptures, and again about the work that they did with their hands. But the old man held his peace through all. When they reached the harbor, they perceived that the old man also was on his way to the abbot Antony. And when they had come to him, the abbot Antony said to them, "Ye

found a good companion for your journey in this old
man." And he also said to the old man, "Thou didst find
good brethren to company thee, Father." Then said the old
man, "Indeed they be good, but their house hath no door.
Whosoever will, may enter into the stable and loose the
ass." Now he said this because whatsoever came into their
hearts, that they spoke with their mouths.

XII

At one time Epiphanius, bishop of Cyprus, sent to the
abbot Hilarion, asking him and saying, "Come that I may
see thee, before I go forth from the body." And when they
had come together and were eating, a portion of fowl was
brought them, and the bishop took it and gave to the abbot
Hilarion. And the old man said to him, "Forgive me,
Father, but from the time that I took this habit, I have
eaten naught that hath been killed." And Epiphanius said to
him, "And I from the time that I took this habit have let no
man sleep that had aught against me, nor have I slept
holding aught against any man." And the old man said to
him, "Forgive me, for thy way of life is greater than
mine."

XIII

The abbot Hyperichius said, "The monk that cannot master
his tongue in time of anger will not be master of the
passions of his body at some other time."

He said again, "It is better to eat flesh and to drink
wine than to eat the flesh of the brethren by backbiting
them."

XIV

An old man had lived long in the desert, and it chanced that a brother came to see him, and found him ill. And he washed his face and made him a meal of the things he had brought with him. And when the old man saw it, he said, "Indeed, brother, I had forgotten what solace men may have in food." He offered him also a cup of wine. And when he saw it, he wept, saying, "I had not thought to drink wine until I died."

XV

Another brother was goaded by lust, and rising at night he made his way to an old man and told him his thoughts, and the old man comforted him. And revived by that comforting he returned to his cell. And again the spirit of lust tempted him, and again he went to the old man. And this happened many times. But the old man did not discountenance him but spoke to him to his profit, saying, "Yield not to the Devil, nor relax thy mind; but rather as often as the Devil troubles thee, come to me, and he shall go buffeted away. For nothing so dispirits the demon of lust as when his assaults are revealed. And nothing so heartens him as when his imaginations are kept secret." So the brother came to him eleven times, confessing his imaginings. And thereafter he said to the old man, "Show love to me, my father, and give me some word." The old man said, "Believe me, my son, if God permitted the thoughts with which my own mind is stung to be transferred to thee, thou wouldst not endure them, but wouldst dash thyself headlong." And by the old man saying this, his great humbleness did quiet the goading of lust in the brother.

XVI

Two brethren made their way to the city to sell their
handiwork; and when in the city they went different ways,
divided one from the other, one of them fell into
fornication. After a while came his brother, saying,
"Brother, let us go back to our cell." But he made answer,
"I am not coming." And the other questioned him, saying,
"Wherefore, Brother?" And he answered, "Because when
thou didst go from me, I ran into temptation, and I sinned
in the flesh." But the other, anxious to help him, began to
tell him, saying, "But so it happened with me; when I was
separated from thee, I, too, ran into fornication. But let us
go and do penance together with all our might, and God
will forgive us that are sinful men." And they came back
to the monastery and told the old men what had befallen
them, and they enjoined on them the penance they must
do. But the one began his penance, not for himself but for
his brother, as if he himself had sinned. And God, seeing
his love and his labor, after a few days revealed to one of
the old men that for the great love of this brother who had
not sinned, he had forgiven the brother who had. And
verily this is to lay down one's soul for one's brother.

XVII

A certain brother who lived solitary was disturbed in mind,
and making his way to the abbot Theodore of Pherme he
told him that he was troubled. The old man said to him,
"Go, humble thy spirit and submit thyself, and live with
other men." So he went away to the mountain and dwelt
with others. And afterwards he came back to the old man
and said to him, "Nor in living with other men have I
found peace." And the old man said, "If thou canst not be
at peace in solitude, nor yet with men, why didst thou will

to be a monk? Was it not that thou shouldst have tribulation? Tell me now, how many years hast thou been in this habit?" And the brother said, "Eight." And the old man said, "Believe me, I have been in this habit seventy years, and not for one day could I find peace; and thou wouldst have peace in eight?"

XVIII

The Fathers used to say, "If temptation befall thee in the place thou dost inhabit, desert not the place in the time of temptation; for if thou dost, wheresoever thou goest, thou shalt find what thou fliest before thee."

XIX

A certain brother while he was in the community was restless and frequently moved to wrath. And he said within himself, "I shall go and live in some place in solitude; and when I have no one to speak to or to hear, I shall be at peace and this passion of anger will be stilled." So he went forth and lived by himself in a cave. One day he filled a jug for himself with water and set it on the ground, but it happened that it suddenly overturned. He filled it a second time, and again it overturned; and he filled it a third time and set it down, and it overturned again. And in a rage he caught up the jug and broke it. Then when he had come to himself, he thought how he had been tricked by the spirit of anger and said, "Behold, here am I alone, and nevertheless he hath conquered me. I shall return to the community, for in all places there is need for struggle and for patience and above all for the help of God." And he arose and returned to his place.

XX

At one time a provincial judge heard of the abbot Moses
and set out into Scete to see him, but the old man heard of
his coming and got up to flee into the marsh. And the
judge with his following met him and questioned him,
saying, "Tell me, old man, where is the cell of the abbot
Moses?" And he said, "Why would you seek him out? This
man is a fool and a heretic." So the judge coming to the
church said to the clergy; "I had heard of the abbot Moses
and came to see him, but lo! we met an old man journeying
into Egypt and asked him where might be the cell of the
abbot Moses, and he said, 'Why do you seek him? He is a
fool and a heretic.'" The clergy, on hearing this, were
perturbed and said, "What was this old man like, who
spoke thus to you of the holy man?" And they said, "He
was an old man, wearing a very ancient garment, tall and
black." And they said, "It is the abbot himself; and because
he did not wish to be seen by you, he told you these things
about himself." And mightily edified, the judge went away.

XXI

The abbot Nisteron the elder was walking in the desert
with a certain brother, and seeing a dragon they fled. And
the brother said to him, "Art thou also afraid, Father?" The
old man replied, "I am not afraid, my son, but it was
expedient that I should flee at sight of the dragon, that I
might not have to fly the spirit of vainglory."

XXII

The holy Syncletica said, "A treasure that is known is
quickly spent; and even so any virtue that is commented on

and made a public show of is destroyed. Even as wax is melted before the face of fire, so is the soul enfeebled by praise and loses the toughness of its virtues."

XXIII

A brother asked the abbot Pastor, saying, "If I should see my brother's fault, is it good to hide it?" The old man said to him, "In what hour we do cover up our brother's sins, God shall cover ours; and in what hour we do betray our brother's shames, in like manner God shall betray our own."

XXIV

An old man said, "Judge not him who is guilty of fornication, if thou art chaste, or thou thyself wilt offend a similar law. For he who said, 'Thou shalt not fornicate,' said also, 'Thou shalt not judge.'"

XXV

The abbot Antony said, "There be some that wear out their bodies with abstinence, but because they have no discretion, they be a great way from God."

XXVI

The abbot Agatho said, "If an angry man were to raise the dead, because of his anger he would not please God."

XXVII

They told of a certain old man that he had lived fifty years neither eating bread nor readily drinking water, and that he said, "I have killed in me lust and avarice and vainglory." The abbot Abraham heard that he said these things, and he came to him and said, "Hast thou spoken thus?" And he answered, "Even so." And the abbot Abraham said, "Behold, thou dost enter thy cell and find upon thy bed a woman; canst thou refrain from thinking that it is a woman?" And he said, "No, but I fight my thoughts so as not to touch that woman." And the abbot Abraham said, "So then, thou has not slain lust, for the passion itself liveth, but it is bound. Again, if thou art walking on the road and seest stones and potsherds, and lying amongst them gold, canst thou think of it but as stones?" And he answered, "No, but I resist my thought so as not to pick it up." And the abbot Abraham said, "So then, passion liveth; but it is bound." And again the abbot Abraham said, "If thou shouldst hear of two brethren, that one loves thee and speaks well of thee, but the other hates thee and disparages thee, and they should come to thee, wouldst thou give them an equal welcome?" And he said, "No, but I should wrest my mind so that I should do as much for him that hated me as for him that loved me." And the abbot Abraham said, "So then these passions live, but by holy men they are in some sort bound."

XXVIII

The abbot Macarius said, "If we dwell upon the harms that have been wrought on us by men, we amputate from our mind the power of dwelling upon God."

XXIX

A brother asked the abbot Pastor, saying, "Trouble has come upon me and I would fain leave this place." And the old man said to him, "For what reason?" And he said, "I have heard tales of a certain brother that do not edify me." And the old man said, "Are the tales true that thou hast heard?" And he said, "Yea, Father, they are true, for the brother who told me is faithful." And he answering said, "He is not faithful that told thee; for if he were faithful, he would never tell thee such things. God heard tell of the men of Sodom, but he believed it not till he went down and saw with his own eyes." But he said, "And I have seen with mine own eyes." The old man heard him and looked upon the ground and picked up a little straw and said to him, "What is this?" And he answered, "A straw." And again the old man gazed at the roof of the cell and said, "What is this?" And he said, "It is the beam that holds up the roof." And the old man said to him, "Take it to thy heart that thy sins are as this beam; the sins of that brother of whom thou dost speak are as this poor straw."

XXX

He said again, "If there be three in one place, and one of them lives the life of holy quiet, and another is ill and gives thanks, and the third tends them with an honest heart, these three are alike, as if their work was one."

XXXI

There came three brethren to a certain old man in Scete, and one of them asked him, saying, "Father, I have committed the Old and New Testaments to memory." And the old man answered and said, "Thou hast filled the air with words." And the second asked him, saying, "I have written the Old and New Testaments with my own hand." But he said to him, "And thou has filled the windows with manuscripts." And the third said, "The grass grows on my hearthstone." And the old man answered and said, "And thou has driven hospitality from thee."

XXXII

Certain old men said, "If thou seest a young man ascending by his own will up to Heaven, catch him by the foot and throw him down upon earth, for it is not expedient for him."

XXXIII

The abbot Moses asked the abbot Silvanus, saying, "Can a man every day make a beginning of the good life?" The abbot Silvanus answered him, "If he be diligent, he can every day and every hour begin the good life anew."

XXXIV

The holy Syncletica said, "Let us live soberly, for through the senses of our body, even though it be against our will, thieves do enter in; for how shall the house not be darkened if the smoke rising without shall find the windows open?"

XXXV

They told of a certain old man that when his thoughts said
to him, "Let be today; thou shalt repent tomorrow," he
would contradict them, saying, "Nay, but I shall repent
today; tomorrow may the will of God be done."

XXXVI

The abbot Cassian said, "We came from Palestine into
Egypt, to one of the Fathers. And he showed us hospitality,
and we said to him, "Wherefore, in welcoming the
brethren doest thou not keep the rule of fasting, as they do
in Palestine?" And he made answer, "Fasting is ever with
me, but I cannot keep you ever here; and though fasting be
indeed useful and necessary, it is a matter of our own
choosing; but love in its fullness the law of God requires at
our hands. So, receiving Christ in you, I must show you
whatever things be of love, with all carefulness; but when I
have sent you away, then may I take up again the rule of
fasting. The children of the bridegroom do not fast while
the bridegroom is with them, but when he is taken from
them, then shall they fast; it is in their own power."

XXXVII

A brother came to a certain solitary; and when he was
going away from him, he said, "Forgive me, Father, for I
have made thee break thy rule." He made answer and said,
"My rule is to receive thee with hospitality and send thee
away in peace."

XXXVIII

One of the old men used to say, "There be some that do
great good, and the devil sends parsimony into their souls
over trifles, so that they lose the merit of all the rest.

XXXIX

At one time there came old men to the abbot Antony, and
the abbot Joseph was with them. And the abbot Antony,
wishing to prove them, brought the discourse to the Holy
Scriptures. And he began to question, beginning with the
younger men, what this or that word might mean. And
each made answer as best he could. But he said to them,
"Ye have not found it yet." After them he said to the abbot
Joseph, "What dost thou say this word might be?" He
answered, "I know not." And the abbot Antony said,
"Verily the abbot Joseph alone hath found the road, who
saith that he doth not know."

XL

They said of the abbot Arsenius that when he was in the
palace none wore finer garments than he; and when he was
in holy living, none was so poorly clad.

XLI

At one time the abbot Arsenius was taking counsel with an
old man of Egypt about his thoughts, and another, seeing
him, said, "Abbot Arsenius, how is it that thou, who art so
great a scholar in the Latin tongue and the Greek, dost take
counsel of this countryman about thy thoughts?" And he

answered, "I have indeed apprehended the learning of the Greeks and the Latins, as this world goes; but the alphabet of this countryman I have not yet been able to learn."

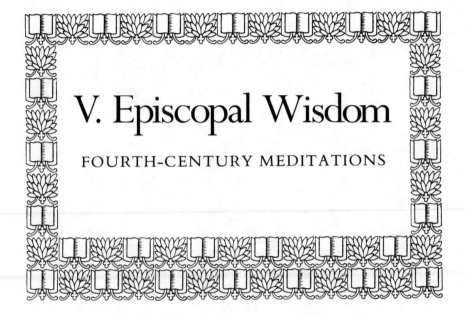

V. Episcopal Wisdom

FOURTH-CENTURY MEDITATIONS

So great a wonder is formed by a word alone.

GREGORY OF NYSSA

WITH the conversion of Constantine and the eleva-
tion of Christianity to the status of Roman state
religion, the same church that remained under siege
at the turn of the fourth century had by the year 325
become the church triumphant. Some Christians, fearing the
corruption of faith, recoiled at this, choosing the desert over the
city. But along with the flowering of Christianity in the desert, the
triumph of the church led to a golden age of theology in the
empire's great cities. The intellectual giants of the fourth
century—both in the artistry of their expression and in the breadth
of their vision—were the leaders, or bishops, of the Christian
Church. Schooled in the finest academics, well versed in the
literature and philosophy of Greece and Rome, figures such as Saint
Ambrose, Saint Gregory of Nazianzus, and Saint Gregory of Nyssa
dominated the intellectual and the spiritual landscape. The following two chapters offer some indication of how the uneasy but
official marriage of classical learning and biblical faith led to the
flourishing of a very different style of Christian meditation than
that of the desert fathers.

Chapter nine contains selections from Saint Ambrose of
Milan's masterpiece, *De Officiis Ministrorum* (On the Duties of the
Clergy). Perhaps best known as Saint Augustine's teacher, Ambrose is a powerful figure in his own right; he was not only a fine
preacher and magnificent stylist but also a pillar of orthodoxy
whose knowledge of Greek as well as Latin led to the bridging of
Eastern and Western theology. Ambrose's *Duties* are patterned after
a treatise of Cicero (*De Officiis*), adapting the latter's treatment of
that which is right or honorable and that which is expedient or
useful, to include not only this world but also the next. At times
this work is reminiscent of another book as well—the *Meditations* of
Marcus Aurelius.

Turning to the East, in chapter ten we offer selections from the
writings of three bishops. Saint Athanasius, bishop of Alexandria
was one of the most influential architects of Christian dogma, as

codified at the Council of Nicaea in 325. He wrote a famous meditation on the Incarnation, from which we have excerpted the final paragraph. Saint Gregory of Nazianzus and Saint Gregory of Nyssa, two of the Cappadocian Fathers (who together were instrumental in developing the doctrine of the trinity), were among the most prolific, artful, and penetrating theologians of their day. The selections from their orations illustrate the way in which speculative philosophy may be combined with practical piety to elevate the mind while nourishing the soul.

NINE

Saint Ambrose's
Duties of the Clergy

THE snare of the enemy is our speech—but that itself is also just as much an enemy to us. Too often we say something that our foe takes hold of, and whereby he wounds us as though by our own sword. How far better it is to perish by the sword of others than by our own!

Accordingly the enemy tests our arms and clashes together his weapons. If he sees that I am disturbed, he implants the points of his darts, so as to raise a crop of quarrels. If I utter an unseemly word, he sets his snare. Then he puts before me the opportunity for revenge as a bait, so that in desiring to be revenged, I may put myself in the snare, and draw the death knot tight for myself. If anyone feels this enemy is near, he ought to give greater heed to his mouth, lest he make room for the enemy; but not many see him. . . . For he who irritates us and does us an injury is committing sin, and wishes us to become like himself.

"ON SILENCE," FROM BOOK 1

I

THERE are two kinds of mental motions. . . . The one has to do with reflection, the other with passion. There is no confusion one with the other, for they are markedly different and unlike. Reflection has to search and as it were to grind out the truth. Passion prompts and stimulates us to do something. Thus by its very nature reflection diffuses tranquility and calm; and passion sends forth the impulse to act. Let us then be ready to allow reflection on good things to enter into our mind, and to make passion submit to reason (if indeed we wish to direct our minds to guard what is seemly), lest desire for anything should shut out reason. Rather let reason test and see what befits virtue.

II

Let us now consider what beseems an active life. We note that there are three things to be regarded in connection with this subject. One is that passion should not resist our reason. In that way only can our duties be brought into line with what is seemly. For if passion yields to reason we can easily maintain what is seemly in our duties. Next, we must take care lest, either by showing greater zeal or less than the matter we take up demands, we look as though we were taking up a small matter with great parade or were treating a great matter with but little care. Thirdly, as regards moderation in our endeavors and works, and also with regard to order in doing things and in the right timing of things, I think that everything should be open and straight forward.

But first comes that which I may call the foundation of all, namely, that our passions should obey our reason.

III

The first source of duty is prudence. For what is more of a duty than to give to the Creator all one's devotion and reverence? This source, however, is drawn off into other virtues. For justice cannot exist without prudence, since it demands no small amount of prudence to see whether a thing is just or unjust. A mistake on either side is very serious. "For he that says a just man is unjust, or an unjust man is just, is accursed with God. Wherefore does justice abound unto the wicked?" says Solomon. Nor, on the other hand, can prudence exist without justice, for piety toward God is the beginning of understanding. On which we notice that this is a borrowed rather than an original idea among the worldly wise, for piety is the foundation of all virtues.

But the piety of justice is first directed toward God; secondly, toward one's country; next, toward parents; lastly, toward all. This, too, is in accordance with the guidance of nature. From the beginning of life, when understanding first begins to be infused into us, we love life as the gift of God, we love our country and our parents; lastly, our companions, with whom we like to associate. Hence arises true love, which prefers others to self, and seeks not its own, wherein lies the preeminence of justice.

It is ingrained in all living creatures, first of all, to preserve their own safety, to guard against what is harmful, to strive for what is advantageous. They seek food and coverts, whereby they may protect themselves from dangers, storms, and sun—all which is a mark of prudence. Next we find that all the different creatures are by nature wont to herd together, at first with fellows of their own class and sort, then also with others. So we see oxen delighted to be in herds, horses in droves, and especially like with like, stags, also, in company with stags . . .

It is clear, then, that these and the remaining virtues are related to one another. For courage, which in war preserves one's country from the barbarians, or at home defends the weak, or comrades from robbers, is full of justice; and to know on what plan to defend and to give help, how to make use of opportunities of time and place, is the part of prudence and moderation, and temperance itself cannot observe due measure without prudence. To know a fit opportunity, and to make return according to what is right, belongs to justice. In all these, too, large-heartedness is necessary, and fortitude of mind, and often of body, so that we may carry out what we wish.

IV

Justice has to do with the society of the human race and the community at large. For that which holds society together is divided into two parts—justice and goodwill, which also is called liberality and kindness. Justice seems to me the loftier, liberality the more pleasing, of the two. The one gives judgment, the other shows goodness.

V

Kindness breaks up into two parts, goodwill and liberality. Kindness to exist in perfection must consist of these two qualities. It is not enough just to wish well; we must also do well. Nor, again, is it enough to do well, unless this springs from a good source, even from a good will. "For God loveth a cheerful giver." If we act unwillingly, what is our reward? Wherefore the Apostle, speaking generally, says: "If I do this thing willingly, I have a reward, but if unwillingly, a dispensation is given unto me." In the Gospel, also, we have received many rules of just liberality.

It is thus a glorious thing to wish well, and to give freely, with the one desire to do good and not to do harm. For if we were to think it our duty to give the means to an extravagant man to live extravagantly, or to an adulterer to pay for his adultery, it would not be an act of kindness, for there would be no goodwill in it. We should be doing harm, not good, to another if we gave him money to aid him in plotting against his country, or in attempting to get together at our expense some abandoned men to attack the Church. Nor, again, does it look like liberality to help one who presses very hardly on widows and orphans, or attempts to seize on their property with any show of violence.

It is no sign of a liberal spirit to extort from one what we give to another, or to gain money unjustly, and then to think it can be well spent, unless we act as Zacchaeus did, and restore fourfold what we have taken from him whom we have robbed, and make up for such heathenish crimes by the zeal of our faith and by true Christian labor. Our liberality must have some sure foundation.

The first thing necessary is to do kindness in good faith, and not to act falsely when the offering is made. Never let us say we are doing more when we are really doing less. What need is there to speak at all? In a promise a cheat lies hid. It is in our power to give what we like. Cheating shatters the foundation and so destroys the work. Did Peter grow angry only so far as to desire that Ananias and his wife should be slain? Certainly not. He wished that others, through knowing their example, should not perish.

Nor is it a real act of liberality if thou givest for the sake of boasting about it, rather than for mercy's sake. Thy inner feelings give the name to thy acts. As it comes forth from thee, so will others regard it. See what a true judge thou hast! He consults with thee how to take up they work, and first of all he questions thy mind. "Let not, " he says, "thy left hand know what thy right hand doth." This does not refer to our actual bodies but means: Let not him who is of one mind with thee, not even thy brother, know what thou doest, lest thou shouldst lose the fruit of thy reward hereafter by seeking here thy price in boastfulness. But that liberality is real where a man hides what he does in silence, and secretly assists the needs of individuals, whom the mouth of the poor, and not his own lips, praises.

VI

Goodwill also is wont to remove the sword of anger. It is also goodwill that makes the wounds of a friend to be better than the willing kisses of an enemy. Goodwill again makes many to become one. For if many are friends, they become one, in whom there is but one spirit and one opinion. We note, too, that in friendship corrections are pleasing. They have their sting, but they cause no pain. We are pierced by the words of blame, but are delighted with the anxiety that goodwill shows.

VII

Let none show himself to be given to flattery, nor to be desirous of flattery from anyone. The one is a mark of artfulness, the other of vanity.

Let no one ever look down on what another, least of all a good man, thinks of him, for thus he learns to give regard to the good. For to disregard the judgment of good men is a sign of conceitedness or of weakness. One of these arises from pride, the other from carelessness.

We ought to be careful never to do anything rashly or carelessly, or anything at all for which we cannot give a reasonable ground. For though a reason for our action is not given to everyone, yet everybody looks into it. Nor, indeed, have we anything whereby we can excuse ourselves. For though there is a sort of natural force in every passion of ours, yet that same passion is subject to reason by the law of nature itself, and is obedient to it. Wherefore it is the duty of a careful watchman so to keep a lookout, that passion may not outrun reason nor utterly forsake it, lest by outstripping it confusion be caused, and reason be shut out, and come to nothing by such desertion. Disquiet destroys consistency. Withdrawal shows cowardice and implies indolence. For when the mind is disquieted

passion spreads wide and far, and in a fierce outburst
endures not the reins of reason and feels not the
management of its driver so as to be turned back.
Wherefore as a rule not only is the soul perturbed and
reason lost, but one's countenance gets inflamed by anger
or by lust, it grows pale with fear, it contains not itself in
pleasure, and cannot bear joy.

When this happens, then that natural judgment and
weight of character is cast aside, and that consistency which
alone in deed and thought can keep up its own authority
and what is seemly, can no longer be retained.

"ON THE VIRTUES," FROM BOOK 1

I

THE regard in which one is held is also very much
enhanced when one rescues a poor man out of the hands
of a powerful one, or saves a condemned criminal from
death; so long as it can be done without disturbance, for
fear that we might seem to be doing it rather for the sake
of showing off than for pity's sake, and so might inflict
severer wounds whilst desiring to heal slighter ones. But if
one has freed a man who is crushed down by the resources
and faction of a powerful person, rather than overwhelmed
by the deserts of his own wickedness, then the witness of a
great and high opinion grows strong.

Hospitality also serves to recommend many. For it is a
kind of open display of kindly feelings; so that the stranger
may not want hospitality, but be courteously received, and
that the door may be open to him when he comes. It is
most seemly in the eyes of the whole world that the
stranger should be received with honor; that the charm of
hospitality should not fail at our table; that we should meet
a guest with ready and free service, and look out for his
arrival.

This especially was Abraham's praise, for he watched at the door of his tent, that no stranger by any chance might pass by. He carefully kept a lookout so as to meet the stranger, and anticipate him, and ask him not to pass by, saying: "My lord, if I have found favor in thy sight, pass not by thy servant." Therefore as a reward for his hospitality, he received the gift of posterity.

Lot also, his nephew, who was near to him not only in relationship but also in virtue, on account of his readiness to show hospitality, turned aside the punishment of Sodom from himself and his family.

A man ought therefore to be hospitable, kind, upright, not desirous of what belongs to another, willing to give up some of his own rights if assailed, rather than to take away another's. He ought to avoid disputes, to hate quarrels. He ought to restore unity and the grace of quietness. When a good man gives up any of his own rights, it is not only a sign of liberality, but is also accompanied by great advantages. To start with, it is no small gain to be free from the cost of a lawsuit. Then it also brings in good results, by an increase of friendship, from which many advantages rise. These become afterwards most useful to the man that can despise a little something at the time.

In all the duties of hospitality kindly feeling must be shown to all, but greater respect must be given to the upright. For: "Whosoever receiveth a righteous man, in the name of a righteous man, shall receive a righteous man's reward," as the Lord has said. Such is the favor in which hospitality stands with God, that not even the draft of cold water shall fail of getting a reward. Thou seest that Abraham, in looking for guests, received God himself to entertain. Thou seest that Lot received the angels. And how dost thou know that when thou receivest men, thou dost not receive Christ? Christ may be in the stranger that comes, for Christ is there in the person of the poor, as he himself says: "I was in prison and thou camest to me; I was naked and thou didst clothe me."

It is sweet, then, to seek not for money but for grace. It is true that this evil has long ago entered into human hearts, so that money stands in the place of honor, and the minds of men are filled with admiration for wealth. Thus love of money sinks in and as it were dries up every kindly duty, so that men consider everything a loss which is spent beyond the usual amount. But even here the holy Scriptures have been on the watch against love of money, that it might prove no cause of hindrance, saying: "Better is hospitality, even though it consisteth only of herbs." And again: "Better is bread in pleasantness with peace." For the Scriptures teach us not to be wasteful, but liberal.

There are two kinds of free giving, one arising from liberality, the other from wasteful extravagance. It is a mark of liberality to receive the stranger, to clothe the naked, to redeem the captives, to help the needy. It is wasteful to spend money on expensive banquets and much wine. Wherefore one reads: "Wine is wasteful, drunkenness is abusive." It is wasteful to spend one's own wealth merely for the sake of gaining the favor of the people. This they do who spend their inheritance on the games of the circus, or on theatrical pieces and gladiatorial shows, or even a combat of wild beasts, just to surpass the fame of their forefathers for these things. All this that they do is but foolish, for it is not right to be extravagant in spending money even on good works.

II

In giving judgment let us have no respect of persons. Favor must be put out of sight, and the case be decided on its merits. Nothing is so great a strain on another's good opinion or confidence, as the fact of our giving away the cause of the weaker to the more powerful in any case that comes before us. The same happens if we are hard on the poor, whilst we make excuses for the rich man when guilty. Men are ready enough to flatter those in high positions, so as not to let them think themselves injured, or to feel vexed as though overthrown. But if thou fearest to give offense then do not undertake to give judgment. If thou art a priest or some cleric do not urge it. It is allowable for thee to be silent in the matter, if it be a money affair, though it is always due to consistency to be on the side of equity. But in the cause of God, where there is danger to the whole Church, it is no small sin to act as though one saw nothing.

III

But what advantage is it to thee to show favor to a rich man? Is it that he is more ready to repay one who loves him? For we generally show favor to those from whom we expect to receive a return of favor. But we ought to think far more of the weak and helpless, because we hope to receive, on behalf of him who has it not, a recompense from the Lord Jesus, who in the likeness of a marriage feast has given us a general representation of virtue. By this he bids us confer benefits rather on those who cannot give them to us in return, teaching us to bid to our feasts and meals, not those who are rich, but those that are poor. For the rich seem to be asked that they may prepare a banquet for us in return; the poor, as they have nothing wherewith to make return, when they receive anything, make the Lord to be our recompense who has offered himself as surety for the poor.

In the ordinary course of things, too, the conferring of a benefit on the poor is of more use than when it is conferred on the rich. The rich man scorns the benefit and is ashamed to feel indebted for a favor. Nay, moreover, whatever is offered to him he takes as due to his merits, as though only a just debt were paid him; or else he thinks it was but given because the giver expected a still greater return to be made him by the rich man. So, in accepting a kindness, the rich man, on that very ground, thinks that he has given more than he ever received. The poor man, however, though he has no money wherewith he can repay, at least shows his gratitude. And herein it is certain that he returns more than he received. For money is paid in coins, but gratitude never fails; money grows less by payment, but gratitude fails when held back, and is preserved when given to others. Next—a thing the rich man avoids—the poor man owns that he feels bound by the debt. He really thinks help has been given him, not that it has been offered in return for his honor. He considers that his children have been again given him, that his life is restored and his family preserved. How much better, then, is it to confer benefits upon the good than on the ungrateful.

"ON RESPECT TO PERSONS," FROM BOOK 2

MY sons, avoid wicked men, guard against the envious. There is this difference between a wicked and an envious man: the wicked man is delighted at his own good fortune, but the envious is tortured at the thought of another's. The former loves evil, the latter hates good. So he is almost more bearable who desires good for himself alone, than he who desires evil for all.

My sons, think before you act, and when you have thought long then do what you consider right. When the opportunity of a praiseworthy death is given let it be seized at once. Glory that is put off flies away and is not easily laid hold of again.

"CLOSING EXHORTATION," FROM BOOK 2

A man who guides himself according to the ruling of nature, so as to be obedient to her, can never injure another. If he injures another, he violates nature, nor will he think that what he has gained is so much an advantage as a disadvantage. And what punishment is worse than the wounds of the conscience within? What judgment harder than that of our hearts, whereby each one stands convicted and accuses himself of the injury that he has wrongfully done against his brother? . . .

The advantage of the individual is the same as that of all, and nothing must be considered advantageous except what is for the general good. For how can one be benefited alone? That which is useless to all is harmful. I certainly cannot think that he who is useless to all can be of use to himself. For if there is one law of nature for all, there is also one state of usefulness for all. And we are bound by the law of nature to act for the good of all. It is not, therefore, right for him who wishes the interests of another to be considered according to nature, to injure him against the law of nature.

Some ask whether a wise man ought in case of a shipwreck to take away a plank from an ignorant sailor? Although it seems better for the common good that a wise man rather than a fool should escape from shipwreck, yet I do not think that a Christian, a just and a wise man, ought to save his own life by the death of another; just as when he meets with an armed robber he cannot return his blows, lest in defending his life he should stain his love toward his neighbor. The verdict on this is plain and clear in the books of the Gospel: "Put up thy sword, for every one that taketh the sword shall perish with the sword." What robber is more hateful than the persecutor who came to kill Christ? But Christ would not be defended from the wounds of the persecutor, for he willed to heal all by his wounds.

Why dost thou consider thyself greater than another, when a Christian man ought to put others before himself, to claim nothing for himself, usurp no honors, claim no reward for his merits? Why, next, art thou not wont to bear thy own troubles rather than to destroy another's advantage? For what is so contrary to nature as not to be content with what one has or to seek what is another's, and to try to get it in shameful ways. For if a virtuous life is in accordance with nature—for God made all things very good—then shameful living must be opposed to it. A virtuous and a shameful life cannot go together, since they are absolutely severed by the law of nature.

"ON CONSCIENCE AND THE LAW OF NATURE," FROM BOOK 3

T E N

The Greek Fathers

FOR the searching of the Scriptures and true knowledge of
them, an honorable life is needed, and a pure soul, and that
virtue which is according to Christ; so that the intellect
guiding its path by it may be able to attain what it desires,
and to comprehend it, insofar as it is accessible to human
nature to learn concerning the Word of God. For without a
pure mind and a modeling of the life after the saints, a man
could not possibly comprehend the words of the saints. For
just as, if a man wished to see the light of the sun, he
would at any rate wipe and brighten his eye, purifying
himself in some sort like what he desires, so that the eye,
thus becoming light, may see the light of the sun; or as, if a
man would see a city or country, he at any rate comes to
the place to see it; thus he that would comprehend the mind
of those who speak of God must needs begin by washing
and cleansing his soul, by his manner of living, and
approach the saints themselves by imitating their works; so
that, associated with them in the conduct of a common life,
he may understand also what has been revealed to them by
God, and thenceforth, as closely knit to them, may escape
the peril of the sinners and their fire at the day of
judgment, and receive what is laid up for the saints in the
kingdom of Heaven, which "eye hath not seen, nor ear
heard, neither have entered into the heart of man,"
whatsoever things are prepared for them that live a virtuous
life, and love the God and Father, in Christ Jesus our Lord:

through whom and with whom be to the Father himself, with the Son himself, in the Holy Spirit, honor and might and glory forever and ever.

SAINT ATHANASIUS,
"INCARNATION OF THE WORD"

LET us become like Christ, since Christ became like us. Let us become God's for his sake, since he for ours became Man. He assumed the worse that he might give us the better; he became poor that we through his poverty might be rich; he took upon him the form of a servant that we might receive back our liberty; he came down that we might be exalted; he was tempted that we might conquer; he was dishonored that he might glorify us; he died that he might save us; he ascended that he might draw to himself us, who were lying low in the fall of sin. Let us give all, offer all, to him who gave himself a ransom and a reconciliation for us. But one can give nothing like oneself, understanding the mystery, and becoming for his sake all that he became for ours.

SAINT GREGORY ON NAZIANZUS, "ORATION 1"

THE nature of God . . . is not the same as that of men; indeed, to speak generally, the nature of divine things is not the same as that of earthly things. They possess unchangeableness and immortality, and absolute being with its consequences, for sure are the properties of things sure. But how is it with what is ours? It is in a state of flux and corruption, constantly undergoing some fresh change. Life

and death, as they are called, apparently so different, are in
a sense resolved into, and successive to, each other. For the
one takes its rise from the corruption which is our mother,
runs its course through the corruption which is the
displacement of all that is present, and comes to an end in
the corruption which is the dissolution of this life; while the
other, which is able to set us free from the ills of this life,
and oftentimes translates us to the life above, is not in my
opinion accurately called death, and is more dreadful in
name than in reality; so that we are in danger of irrationally
being afraid of what is not fearful, and courting as
preferable what we really ought to fear. There is one life, to
look to life. There is one death, sin, for it is the destruction
of the soul. But all else, of which some are proud, is a
dream vision, making sport of realities, and a series of
phantasms which lead the soul astray. If this be our
condition . . . we shall neither be proud of life nor greatly
hurt by death.

SAINT GREGORY OF NAZIANZUS, "ORATION 20"

DOES the sense of separation cause you pain? Let hope
cheer you. Is widowhood grievous to you? Yet it is not so
to him. And what is the good of love, if it gives itself easy
things, and assigns the more difficult to its neighbor? And
why should it be grievous at all, to one who is soon to pass
away? The appointed day is at hand, the pain will not last
long. Let us not, by ignoble reasonings, make a burden of
things which are really light. We have endured a great
loss—because the privilege we enjoyed was great. Loss is
common to all, such a privilege to few. Let us rise superior
to the one thought by the consolation of the other. For it is
more reasonable, that that which is better should win the
day. You have borne, in a most brave, Christian spirit, the

loss of children, who were still in their prime and qualified
for life; bear also the laying aside of his aged body by one
who was weary of life, although his vigor of mind
preserved for him his senses unimpaired. Do you want
someone to care for you? Where is your Isaac, whom he
left behind for you, to take his place in all respects? Ask of
him small things, the support of his hand and service, and
requite him with greater things, a mother's blessing and
prayers, and the consequent freedom. Are you vexed at
being admonished? I praise you for it. For you have
admonished many whom your long life has brought under
your notice. What I have said can have no application to
you, who are so truly wise; but let it be a general medicine
of consolation for mourners, so that they may know that
they are mortals following mortals to the grave.

SAINT GREGORY OF NAZIANZUS, "ORATION 21"

WHO poured forth the air, that great and abundant
wealth, not measured to men by their rank or fortunes; not
restrained by boundaries; not divided out according to
people's ages; but like the distribution of the Manna,
received in sufficiency, and valued for its equality of
distribution; the chariot of the winged creation; the seat of
the winds; the moderator of the seasons; the quickener of
living things, or rather the preserver of natural life in the
body; in which bodies have their being, and by which we
speak; in which is the light and all that it shines upon, and
the sight which flows through it? And mark, if you please,
what follows. I cannot give to the air the whole empire of
all that is thought to belong to the air. What are the
storehouses of the winds? What are the treasuries of the
snow? Who, as Scripture hath said, hath begotten the drops
of dew? Out of whose womb came the ice? And who

bindeth the waters in the clouds, and, fixing part in the clouds (O marvel!) held by his Word though its nature is to flow, poureth out the rest upon the face of the whole earth, and scattereth it abroad in due season, and in just proportions, and neither suffereth the whole substance of moisture to go out free and uncontrolled (for sufficient was the cleansing in the days of Noah; and he who cannot lie is not forgetful of his own covenant) . . . nor yet restraineth it entirely that we should not again stand in need of an Elias to bring the drought to an end. If he shall shut up Heaven, it saith, who shall open it? If he open the floodgates, who shall shut them up? Who can bring an excess or withhold a sufficiency of rain, unless he govern the universe by his own measures and balances? What scientific laws, pray, can you lay down concerning thunder and lightning, O you who thunder from the earth, and cannot shine with even little sparks of truth? To what vapors from earth will you attribute the creation of cloud, or is it due to some thickening of the air, or pressure or crash of clouds of excessive rarity, so as to make you think the pressure the cause of the lightning, and the crash that which makes the thunder? Or what compression of wind having no outlet will account to you for the lightning by its compression, and for the thunder by its bursting out?

Now if you have in your thought passed through the air and all the things of air, reach with me to Heaven and the things of Heaven. And let faith lead us rather than reason, if at least you have learnt the feebleness of the latter in matters nearer to you, and have known reason by knowing the things that are beyond reason, so as not to be altogether on the earth or of the earth, because you are ignorant even of your ignorance.

Who spread the sky around us, and set the stars in order? Or rather, first, can you tell me, of your own knowledge of the things in heaven, what are the sky and the stars; you who know not what lies at your very feet, and cannot even take the measure of yourself, and yet must busy yourself about what is above your nature, and gape at the illimitable? For, granted that you understand orbits and periods, and waxings and wanings, and settings and risings, and some degrees and minutes, and all the other things which make you so proud of your wonderful knowledge; you have not arrived at comprehension of the realities themselves, but only at an observation of some movement, which, when confirmed by longer practice, and drawing the observations of many individuals into one generalization, and thence deducing a law, has acquired the name of Science (just as the lunar phenomena have become generally known to our sight), being the basis of this knowledge. But if you are very scientific on this subject, and have a just claim to admiration, tell me what is the cause of this order and this movement. How came the sun to be a beacon-fire to the whole world, and to all eyes like the leader of some chorus, concealing all the rest of the stars by his brightness, more completely than some of them conceal others. The proof of this is that they shine against him, but he outshines them and does not even allow it to be perceived that they rose simultaneously with him, fair as a bridegroom, swift and great as a giant—for I will not let his praises be sung from any other source than my own Scriptures—so mighty in strength that from one end to the other of the world he embraces all things in his heat, and there is nothing hid from the feeling thereof, but it fills both every eye with light, and every embodied creature with heat; warming, yet not burning, by the gentleness of its temper, and the order of its movement, present to all, and equally embracing all.

SAINT GREGORY NAZIANZUS,
"THE SECOND THEOLOGICAL ORATION"

GOD always was, and always is, and always will be. Or rather, God always is. For was and will be are fragments of our time, and of changeable nature, but he is Eternal Being. And this is the name that he gives to himself when giving the oracle to Moses in the mount. For in himself he sums up and contains all Being, having neither beginning in the past nor end in the future; like some great Sea of Being, limitless and unbounded, transcending all conception of time and nature, only adumbrated by the mind, and that very dimly and scantily . . . not by his essentials, but by his environment; one image being got from one source and another from another, and combined into some sort of presentation of the truth, which escapes us before we have caught it, and takes to flight before we have conceived it, blazing forth upon our Master part, even when that is cleansed, as the lightning flash which will not stay its course, does upon our sight . . . in order as I conceive by that part of it which we can comprehend to draw us to itself (for that which is altogether incomprehensible is outside the bounds of hope, and not within the compass of endeavor), and by that part of it which we cannot comprehend to move our wonder, and as an object of wonder to become more an object of desire, and being desired to purify, and by purifying to make us like God; so that when we have thus become like himself, God may, to use a bold expression, hold converse with us as gods, being united to us, and that perhaps to the same extent as he already knows those who are known to him. The Divine Nature then is boundless and hard to understand; and all that we can comprehend of him is his boundlessness.

SAINT GREGORY NAZIANZUS,
"ON THE THEOPHANY, OR BIRTHDAY OF CHRIST"

DIVINE beauty is not adorned with any shape or
endowment of form, by any beauty of color, but is
contemplated as excellence in unspeakable bliss. As then
painters transfer human forms to their pictures by the
means of certain colors, laying on their copy the proper and
corresponding tints, so that the beauty of the original may
be accurately transferred to the likeness, so I would have
you understand that our Maker also, painting the portrait to
resemble his own beauty, by the addition of virtues, as it
were with colors, shows in us his own sovereignty; and
manifold and varied are the tints, so to say, by which his
true form is portrayed; not red, or white, or the blending
of these, whatever it may be called, nor a touch of black
that paints the eyebrow and the eye, and shades, by some
combination, the depressions in the figure, and all such arts
which the hands of painters contrive, but instead of these,
purity, freedom from passion, blessedness, alienation from
all evil, and all those attributes of the like kind which help
to form in men the likeness of God, with such hues as these
did the Maker of his own image mark our nature.

   And if you were to examine the other points also by
which the Divine beauty is expressed, you will find that to
them, too, the likeness in the image which we present is
perfectly preserved. The Godhead is mind and word: for
"in the beginning was the Word," and the followers of Paul
"have the mind of Christ" which "speaks" in them;
humanity, too, is not far removed from these: you see in
yourself word and understanding, an imitation of the very
Mind and Word. Again, God is love, and the fount of love;
for this the great John declares that "love is of God," and
"God is love"; the Fashioner of our nature has made this to
be our feature too: for "hereby," he says, "shall all men
know that ye are my disciples, if ye love one
another"—thus, if this be absent, the whole stamp of the
likeness is transformed. The Deity beholds and hears all

things, and searches all things out; you, too, have the power of apprehension of things by means of sight and hearing and the understanding that inquires into things and searches them out.

SAINT GREGORY OF NYSSA, "ON THE MAKING OF MAN"

HOW mean and how unworthy of the majesty of man are the fancies of some heathen writers, who magnify humanity, as they supposed, by their comparison of it to this world! For they say that man is a little world, composed of the same elements with the universe. Those who bestow on human nature such praise as this by a high-sounding name, forget that they are dignifying man with the attributes of the gnat and the mouse; for they, too, are composed of these four elements—because assuredly about the animated nature of every existing thing we behold a part, greater or less, of those elements without which it is not natural that any sensitive being should exist. What great thing is there, then, in man's being accounted a representation and likeness of the world—of the Heaven that passes away, of the earth that changes, of all things that they contain, which pass away with the departure of that which compasses them round?

How, then, is man, this mortal, passible, short-lived being, the image of that nature which is immortal, pure, and everlasting? The true answer to this question, indeed, perhaps only the very Truth knows; but this is what we, tracing out the truth so far as we are capable by conjectures and inferences, apprehend concerning the matter. Neither does the word of God lie when it says that man was made in the image of God, nor is the pitiable suffering of man's nature like to the blessedness of the impassible Life; for if anyone were to compare our nature with God, one of two things must needs be allowed in order that the definition of the likeness may be apprehended in both cases in the same terms—either that the Deity is passible or that humanity is impassible. But if neither the Deity is passible nor our nature free from passion, what other account remains whereby we may say that the word of God speaks truly, which says that man was made in the image of God?

SAINT GREGORY OF NYSSA, "ON THE MAKING OF MAN"

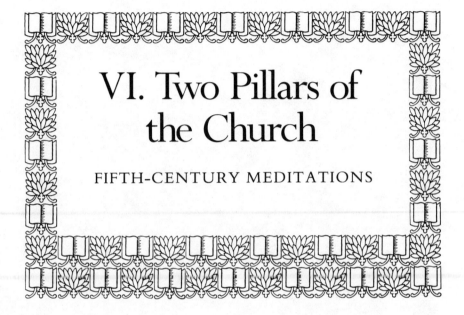

VI. Two Pillars of
the Church

FIFTH-CENTURY MEDITATIONS

If thou knowest how to meditate wisely on these matters,
thou wilt admire the Being who fixed these
immovable boundaries even from the beginning.

SAINT JOHN CHRYSOSTOM

THE apogee of fifth-century meditative Christian literature comes in the West with the writings of Saint Augustine, bishop of Hippo, and in the East with those of Saint John Chrysostom, patriarch of Constantinople. The works of each fill many volumes, even as their works on behalf of orthodoxy and Christian community distinguish them above all others of their generation.

Chapter eleven opens with a selection from Augustine's *Enchiridion,* a manual for spiritual discipline, similar in some ways to the earliest meditative discourses and somewhat later instructional works included in previous chapters. Here he reaffirms a recurring theme: meditation is not a philosophical indulgence but has profound ethical consequences. In Augustine's case, he first poses the question for his reader, then gently, but surely leads him or her toward the answers. We also include several meditations selected from Augustine's writings on the Psalms, preceded by a brief excerpt from *On Christian Doctrine,* which helps to explain his exegetical approach (first to consider "things" in themselves and then to ponder their "significance"). In reflecting on the Psalms, Augustine takes a brief passage, sometimes only a phrase, then proceeds to offer the reader a guided meditation into its meaning, often drawing from other bits of Scripture for further illumination. We close with four representative excerpts from Augustine's homilies, each of which underscores his debt to Saint Ambrose, as can be seen from a comparison between these brief passages and Ambrose's *Duties.*

Saint John Chrysostom, the most noted orator of his time, is to the Eastern Church what Saint Augustine is to the Church in the West. Unlike Augustine, he was wary of allegorical interpretations (the recognition of "things" as "signs"), but far more than his western counterpart, Chrysostom emphasized the practical application of the Scriptures to people's daily lives.

Chapter twelve opens with selections from four homilies included in Chrysostom's collection, *Concerning the Statues,* and concludes with a representative sampling of meditations from his other writings. Note especially his didactic use of familiar things— horses, ships, carpenter shops, fishermen, vines—not so much derivative of Jesus' parables but rather imitative of them. The concreteness of Saint John Chrysostom's images guaranteed that they would be memorable; it also ensured that his teachings would be accessible to all—lay person and scholar alike.

ELEVEN

Saint Augustine
of Hippo

ALL things that exist seeing that the Creator of them all is
supremely good, are themselves good. But because they are
not, like their Creator, supremely and unchangeably good,
their good may be diminished and increased. But for good
to be diminished is an evil, although, however much it may
be diminished, it is necessary, if the being is to continue,
that some good should remain to constitute the being. For
however small or of whatever kind the being may be, the
good which makes it a being cannot be destroyed without
destroying the being itself. An uncorrupted nature is justly
held in esteem. But if, still further, it be incorruptible, it is
undoubtedly considered of still higher value. When it is
corrupted, however, its corruption is an evil, because it is
deprived of some sort of good. For if it be deprived of no
good, it receives no injury; but it does receive injury,
therefore it is deprived of good. Therefore, so long as a
being is in process of corruption, there is in it some good
of which it is being deprived; and if a part of the being
should remain which cannot be corrupted, this will
certainly be an incorruptible being, and accordingly the
process of corruption will result in the manifestation of this
great good. But if it do not cease to be corrupted, neither
can it cease to possess good of which corruption may
deprive it. But if it should be thoroughly and completely

consumed by corruption, there will then be no good left, because there will be no being. Wherefore corruption can consume the good only by consuming the being. Every being, therefore, is a good; a great good, if it cannot be corrupted; a little good, if it can; but in any case, only the foolish or ignorant will deny that it is a good. And if it be wholly consumed by corruption, then the corruption itself must cease to exist, as there is no being left in which it can dwell.

THE ENCHIRIDION

IT is a comparatively small thing to wish well to, or even to do good to, a man who has done no evil to you. It is a much higher thing, and is the result of the most exalted goodness, to love your enemy, and always to wish well to, and when you have the opportunity, to do good to, the man who wishes you ill and, when he can, does you harm. This is to obey the command of God: "Love your enemies, do good to them that hate you, and pray for them which persecute you." But seeing that this is a frame of mind only reached by the perfect sons of God, and that though every believer ought to strive after it, and by prayer to God and earnest struggling with himself endeavor to bring his soul up to this standard, yet a degree of goodness so high can hardly belong to so great a multitude as we believe are heard when they use this petition, "Forgive us our debts, as we forgive our debtors"; in view of all this, it cannot be doubted that the implied undertaking is fulfilled if a man, though he has not yet attained to loving his enemy, yet, when asked by one who has sinned against him to forgive him his sin, does forgive him from his heart. For he certainly desires to be himself forgiven when he prays, "as

we forgive our debtors," that is, Forgive us our debts when
we beg forgiveness, as we forgive our debtors when they
beg forgiveness from us.

Now, he who asks forgiveness of the man against
whom he has sinned, being moved by his sin to ask
forgiveness, cannot be counted an enemy in such a sense
that it should be as difficult to love him now as it was
when he was engaged in active hostility. And the man who
does not from his heart forgive him who repents of his sin,
and asks forgiveness, need not suppose that his own sins are
forgiven of God. For the Truth cannot lie. And what reader
or hearer of the Gospel can have failed to notice that the
same person who said, "I am the Truth," taught us also
this form of prayer; and in order to impress this particular
petition deeply upon our minds, said, "For if ye forgive
men their trespasses, your heavenly Father will also forgive
you; but if ye forgive not men their trespasses, neither will
your Father forgive your trespasses"? The man whom the
thunder of this warning does not awaken is not asleep, but
dead; and yet so powerful is that voice that it can awaken
even the dead.

THE ENCHIRIDION

WHEN there is a question as to whether a man is good,
one does not ask what he believes, or what he hopes, but
what he loves. For the man who loves aright no doubt
believes and hopes aright; whereas the man who has not
love believes in vain, even though his beliefs are true; and
hopes in vain, even though the objects of his hope are a real
part of true happiness; unless, indeed, he believes and hopes
for this, that he may obtain by prayer the blessing of love.
For, although it is not possible to hope without love, it

may yet happen that a man does not love that which is necessary to the attainment of his hope; as, for example, if he hopes for eternal life (and who is there that does not desire this?) and yet does not love righteousness, without which no one can attain to eternal life. Now this is the true faith of Christ which the apostle speaks of, "which worketh by love"; and if there is anything that it does not yet embrace in its love, asks that it may receive, seeks that it may find, and knocks that it may be opened unto it. For faith obtains through prayer that which the law commands. For without the gift of God, that is, without the Holy Spirit, through whom love is shed abroad in our hearts, the law can command, but it cannot assist; and, moreover, it makes a man a transgressor, nor he can no longer excuse himself on the plea of ignorance. Now carnal lust reigns where there is not the love of God.

THE ENCHIRIDION

ALL instruction is either about things or about signs; but things are learnt by means of signs. I now use the word "thing" in a strict sense, to signify that which is never employed as a sign of anything else; for example, wood, stone, cattle, and other things of that kind. Not, however, the wood which we read Moses cast into the bitter waters to make them sweet, nor the stone which Jacob used as a pillow, nor the ram which Abraham offered up instead of his son; for these, though they are things, are also signs of other things. There are signs of another kind, those which are never employed except as signs; for example, words. No one uses words except as signs of something else; and hence may be understood what I call signs: those things, to wit, which are used to indicate something else.

Accordingly, every sign is also a thing; for what is not a thing is nothing at all. Every thing, however, is not also a sign. And so, in regard to this distinction between things and signs, I shall, when I speak of things, speak in such a way that even if some of them may be used as signs also, that will not interfere with the division of the subject according to which I am to discuss things first and signs afterwards.

ON CHRISTIAN DOCTRINE

"IF I have beheld iniquity in my heart, may not the Lord hearken" (ver. 18). Consider now, brethren, how easily, how daily men blushing for fear of men do censure iniquities; he hath done ill, he hath done basely, a villain the fellow is . . . See whether thou beholdest no iniquity in thy heart, whether perchance that which thou censurest in another, thou art meditating to do, and therefore against him dost exclaim, not because he hath done it, but because he hath been found out. Return to thyself, within be to thyself a judge. Behold in thy hid chamber, in the very inmost recess of the heart, where thou and he that seeth are alone, there let iniquity be displeasing to thee, in order that thou mayest be pleasing to God. Do not regard it, that is, do not love it, but rather despise it, that is, condemn it, and turn away from it. Whatever pleasing thing it hath promised to allure thee to sin; whatever grievous thing it hath threatened, to drive thee on to evildoing; all is naught, all passeth away; it is worthy to be despised, in order that it may be trampled upon; not to be eyed lest it be accepted.

ON PSALM 66

"Every soul that is blessed is simple," not cleaving to things earthly nor with glued wings groveling, but beaming with the brightness of virtues, on the twin wings of twin love doth spring into the free air; and seeth how from her is withdrawn that whereon she was treading, not that whereon she was resting, and she saith securely, "The Lord hath given, the Lord hath taken away; as it hath pleased the Lord, so hath been done: be the name of the Lord blessed."

ON PSALM 67

"For he shall speak peace unto his people." The voice of Christ, then, the voice of God, is peace: it calleth unto peace. Ho! it saith, whosoever are not yet in peace, love ye peace: for what can ye find better from me than peace? What is peace? Where there is no war. What is this, where there is no war? Where there is no contradiction, where there is no resistance, nothing to oppose. Consider if we are yet there: consider if there is not now a conflict with the Devil, if all the saints and faithful ones wrestle not with the prince of demons. And how do they wrestle with him whom they see not? They wrestle with their own desires, by which he suggests unto them sins; and by not consenting to what he suggests, though they are not conquered, yet they fight. Therefore there is not yet peace where there is fighting. . . . Whatever we provide for our refreshment, there again we find weariness. Art thou hungry? one asks thee; thou answerest, I am. He places food before thee for thy refreshment; continue thou to use it, for thou hadst need of it; yet in continuing that which thou needest for refreshment, therein findest thou weariness. By long sitting thou wast tired; thou risest and refreshest thyself by walking; continue that relief, and by

much walking thou art wearied; again thou wouldest sit
down. Find me anything by which thou art refreshed,
wherein if thou continue thou dost not again become
weary. What peace, then, is that which men have here,
opposed by so many troubles, desires, wants, wearinesses?
This is no true, no perfect peace. What will be perfect
peace? "This corruptible must put on incorruption, and this
mortal must put on immortality." . . . Persevere in eating
much; this itself will kill thee. Persevere in fasting much; by
this thou wilt die. Sit continually, being resolved not to rise
up; by this thou wilt die. Be always walking so as never to
take rest; by this thou wilt die. Watch continually, taking
no sleep; by this thou wilt die. Sleep continually, never
watching; thus too thou wilt die. When therefore death
shall be swallowed up in victory, these things shall no
longer be; there will be full and eternal peace. We shall be
in a city, of which, brethren, when I speak I find it hard to
leave off, especially when offenses wax common. Who
would not long for that city whence no friend goeth out,
whither no enemy entereth, where is no tempter, no
seditious person, no one dividing God's people, no one
wearying the Church in the service of the Devil; since the
prince himself of all such is cast into eternal fire, and with
him those who consent unto him, and who have no will to
retire from him? There shall be peace made pure in the sons
of God, all loving one another, seeing one another full of
God, since God shall be all in all. We shall have God as our
common object of vision, God as our common possession,
God as our common peace. For whatever there is which he
now giveth unto us, he himself shall be unto us instead of
his gifts; this will be full and perfect peace. This he
speaketh unto his people; this it was which he would
hearken unto who said, "I will hearken what the Lord God
will say unto me, for he shall speak peace unto His people,
and to his saints, and unto those who turn their hearts unto
him." Lo, my brethren, do ye wish that unto you should

belong that peace which God uttereth? Turn your heart
unto him, not unto me, or unto that one, or unto any man.
For whatever man would turn unto himself the hearts of
men, he falleth with them. Which is better, that thou fall
with him unto whom thou turnest thyself, or that thou
stand with him with whom thou turnest thyself? Our joy,
our peace, our rest, the end of all troubles, is none but
God; blessed are "they that turn their hearts unto him."

ON PSALM 85

LET my heart be glad, so that it may fear thy name."
There is then fear in gladness. How can there be gladness,
if fear? Is not fear wont to be painful? There will hereafter
be gladness without fear, now gladness with fear; for not
yet is there perfect security, nor perfect gladness. If there is
no gladness, we faint; if full security, we rejoice wrongly.
Therefore may he both sprinkle on us gladness, and strike
fear into us, that by the sweetness of gladness he may lead
us to the abode of security; by giving us fear, may cause us
not to rejoice wrongly, and to withdraw from the way.
Therefore saith the Psalm: "Serve the Lord in fear, and
rejoice unto him with trembling"; so also saith the Apostle
Paul; "Work out your own salvation with fear and
trembling; for it is God that worketh in you." Whatever
prosperity comes then, my brethren, is rather to be feared;
those things which ye think to be prosperous, are rather
temptations. An inheritance cometh, there cometh wealth,
there is an abundant overflow of some happiness; these are
temptations: take care that they corrupt you not.

ON PSALM 86

"MY truth also and my mercy is with him." All the paths of the Lord are mercy and truth. Remember, as much as ye can, how often these two attributes are urged upon us, that we render them back to God. For as he showed us mercy that he might blot out our sins, and truth in fulfilling his promises; so also we, walking in his path, ought to give back to him mercy and truth; mercy, in pitying the wretched; truth, in not judging unjustly. Let not truth rob you of mercy, nor mercy hinder truth; for if through mercy you shall have judged contrary to truth, or by rigorous truth shall have forgotten mercy, you will not be walking in the path of God, where "mercy and truth meet together."

ON PSALM 89

"O sing unto the Lord a new song; sing unto the Lord, all the earth." If all the earth singeth a new song, it is thus building while it singeth; the very act of singing is building, but only if it singeth not the old song. The lust of the flesh singeth the old song; the love of God singeth the new. . . . Hear why it is a new song: the Lord saith, "A new commandment I give unto you, that ye love one another." The whole earth then singeth a new song: there the house of God is built. All the earth is the house of God. If all the earth is the house of God, he who clingeth not to all the earth is a ruin, not a house; that old ruin whose shadow that ancient temple represented. For there what was old was destroyed, that what was new might be built up.

ON PSALM 96

"FOR the Lord is pleasant" (ver. 4). Think not that ye faint in praising him. Your praise of him is like food: the more ye praise him, the more ye acquire strength, and he whom ye praise becometh the more sweet.

ON PSALM 101

"I will satisfy her poor with bread"; what meaneth this, brethren? Let us be poor, and we shall then be satisfied. Many who trust in the world, and are proud, are Christians; they worship Christ but are not satisfied; for they have been satisfied and abound in their pride. Of such it is said, "Our soul is filled with the scornful reproof of the wealthy and with the despitefulness of the proud. These have abundance, and therefore eat, but are not satisfied. And what is said of them in the Psalm? "All such as be fat upon the earth have eaten and worshiped." They worship Christ, they venerate Christ, they pray unto Christ; but they are not satisfied with his wisdom and righteousness. Wherefore? Because they are not poor. For the poor, that is the humble in heart, the more they hunger, the more they eat; and the more empty they are of the world, the more hungry they are. He who is full refuseth whatsoever thou wilt give him, because he is full. Give me one who hungereth; give me one of whom it is said, "Blessed are they that hunger and thirst after righteousness, for they shall be filled."

ON PSALM 132

THE patience of man, which is right and laudable and worthy of the name of virtue, is understood to be that by which we tolerate evil things with an even mind, that we may not with a mind uneven desert good things, through which we may arrive at better. Wherefore the impatient, while they will not suffer ills, effect not a deliverance from ills, but only the suffering of heavier ills. Whereas the patient who choose rather by not committing to bear, than by not bearing to commit, evil, both make lighter what through patience they suffer, and also escape worse ills in which through impatience they would be sunk. But those good things which are great and eternal they lose not, while to the evils which be temporal and brief they yield not.

ON PATIENCE

WHO can either be prepared to bear injuries from the weak, in as far as it is profitable for their salvation; and to choose rather to suffer more injustice from another than to repay what he has suffered; to give to everyone that asketh anything from him, either what he asks, if it is in his possession, and if it can rightly be given, or good advice, or to manifest a benevolent disposition, and not to turn away from him who desires to borrow; to love his enemies, to do good to those who hate him, to pray for those who persecute him; who, I say, does these things, but the man who is fully and perfectly merciful? And with that counsel misery is avoided, by the assistance of him who says, "I desire mercy, and not sacrifice." "Blessed," therefore, "are the merciful: for they shall obtain mercy."

COMMENTARY ON THE SERMON ON THE MOUNT

T W E L V E

Saint John Chrysostom

"Night unto night sheweth knowledge." If thou knowest how to meditate wisely on these matters, thou wilt admire the Being who fixed these immovable boundaries even from the beginning. Let the avaricious hear these things; and those who are coveting the wealth of others; and let them imitate the equality of the day and night. Let those who are puffed up and high-minded also hear; and those who are unwilling to concede the first places to others! The day gives place to the night, and does not invade the territory of others! But thou, whilst always enjoying honor, canst thou not bear to share it with thy brethren? Consider also with me the wisdom of the Lawgiver. In winter he hath ordered that the night should be long; when the germs are tender, and require more coolness; and are unable to sustain the hotter rays of the sun; but when they are somewhat grown, the day again increases with them, and becomes then the longest, when the fruit has now attained ripeness. And this is a beneficial arrangement not only for seeds but for our bodies. For since during winter, the sailor and the pilot, and the traveler and the soldier and the farmer sit down for the most part at home, fettered by the frost; and the season is one of idleness; God hath appointed that the greater part of this time should be consumed in night, in order that the length of the day might not be superfluous, when men were unable to do anything. Who can describe the perfect order of the seasons; and how these, like some virgins dancing in a circle, succeed one another with the happiest harmony; and how those who are in the middle cease not to pass over to the opposite ones with a gradual and noiseless transition? Therefore, neither are we overtaken by the summer immediately after winter; nor by the winter immediately after the summer; but midway the spring is interposed; that while we gently and gradually take up one season after the other, we may have our bodies hardened to encounter the summer heat without uneasiness. For since sudden changes to opposite extremes are productive of the worst injury and disease, God hath contrived that after winter we should take up the spring, and after the spring the summer; and after the summer the autumn; and thus transport us to winter, so that these changes from seasons which are opposite should come upon us harmlessly and by degrees, through the aid of intermediate ones. Who then is so wretched and pitiable that beholding the heavens; and beholding sea, and land; and beholding this exact adjustment of the seasons, and the unfailing order of day and night, he can think that these things happen of their own accord, instead of adoring him who hath arranged them all with a corresponding wisdom!

HOMILY 9, "CONCERNING THE STATUES"

DOST thou not perceive how this body wastes away, withers, and perishes after the secession of the soul, and each of the elements thereof returns to its own appointed place? This very same thing, indeed, would also happen to the world if the Power which always governs it had left it devoid of its own providence. For if a ship does not hold together without a pilot, but soon founders, how could the

world have held together so long a time if there was no one
governing its course? And that I may not enlarge, suppose
the world to be a ship; the earth to be placed below as the
keel; the sky to be the sail; men to be the passengers; the
subjacent abyss, the sea. How is it, then, that during so
long a time, no shipwreck has taken place? Now let a ship
go one day without a pilot and crew, and thou wilt see it
straightway foundering! But the world, though subsisting
now five thousand years, and many more, hath suffered
nothing of the kind. But why do I talk of a ship? Suppose
one hath pitched a small hut in the vineyards; and when the
fruit is gathered, leaves it vacant; it stands, however, scarce
two or three days, but soon goes to pieces, and tumbles
down! Could not a hut stand without superintendence?
How then could the workmanship of a world, so fair and
marvelous; the laws of the night and day; the interchanging
dances of the seasons; the course of nature checkered and
varied as it is in every way throughout the earth, the sea,
the sky; in plants, and in animals that fly, swim, walk,
creep; and in the race of men, far more dignified than any
of these, continue yet unbroken, during so long a period,
without some kind of providence? But in addition to what
has been said, follow me whilst I enumerate the meadows,
the gardens, the various tribes of flowers; all sorts of herbs,
and their uses; their odors, forms, disposition, yea, but
their very names; the trees which are fruitful, and which are
barren; the nature of metals—and of animals—in the sea, or
on the land; of those that swim, and those that traverse the
air; the mountains, the forests, the groves; the meadow
below, and the meadow above; for there is a meadow on
the earth, and a meadow, too, in the sky; the various
flowers of the stars; the rose below, and the rainbow above!
Would you have me point out also the meadow of birds?
Consider the variegated body of the peacock, surpassing
every dye, and the fowls of purple plumage. Contemplate
with me the beauty of the sky; how it has been preserved

so long without being dimmed; and remains as bright and clear as if it had been only fabricated today; moreover, the power of the earth, how its womb has not become effete by bringing forth during so long a time! Contemplate with me the fountains; how they burst forth and fail not, since the time they were begotten, to flow forth continually throughout the day and night! Contemplate with me the sea, receiving so many rivers, yet never exceeding its measure! But how long shall we pursue things unattainable! It is fit, indeed, that over every one of these which has been spoken of, we should say, "O Lord, how hast thou magnified thy works; in wisdom hast thou made them all."

HOMILY 10, "CONCERNING THE STATUES"

IF thou desirest joy, seek not after riches, nor bodily health, nor glory, nor power, nor luxury, nor sumptuous tables, nor vestures of silk, nor costly lands, nor houses splendid and conspicuous, nor anything else of that kind; but pursue that spiritual wisdom which is according to God, and take hold of virtue; and then naught of the things which are present, or which are expected, will be able to sadden thee. Why do I say to sadden? Verily, the things that make others sad will prove to thee an accession of pleasure. For scourges, and death, and losses, and slanders, and the being evil entreated, and all such things, when they are brought upon us for God's sake, and spring from this root, will bring into our souls much pleasure. For no one will be able to make us miserable if we do not make ourselves such; nor, on the other hand, blessed if we do not make ourselves such, following up the grace of God.

HOMILY 18, "CONCERNING THE STATUES"

WHAT is the virtue of a horse? Is it to have a bridle studded with gold and girths to match, and a band of silken threads to fasten the housing, and clothes wrought in divers colors and gold tissue, and head gear studded with jewels, and locks of hair plaited with gold cord? Or is it to be swift and strong in its legs, and even in its paces, and to have hoofs suitable to a well-bred horse, and courage fitted for long journies and warfare, and to be able to behave with calmness in the battlefield, and if a rout takes place to save its rider? Is it not manifest that these are the things which constitute the virtue of the horse, not the others? Again, what should you say was the virtue of asses and mules? Is it not the power of carrying burdens with contentment, and accomplishing journies with ease, and having hoofs like rock? Shall we say that their outside trappings contribute anything to their own proper virtue? By no means. And what kind of vine shall we admire? One which abounds in leaves and branches, or one which is laden with fruit? Or what kind of virtue do we predicate of an olive? Is it to have large boughs, and great luxuriance of leaves, or to exhibit an abundance of its proper fruit dispersed over all parts of the tree? Well, let us act in the same way in the case of human beings also; let us determine what is the virtue of man, and let us regard that alone as an injury, which is destructive to it. What, then, is the virtue of man? Not riches that thou shouldest fear poverty, nor health of body that thou shouldest dread sickness, nor the opinion of the public, that thou shouldest view an evil reputation with alarm, nor life simply for its own sake, that death should be terrible to thee, nor liberty that thou shouldest avoid servitude; but carefulness in holding true doctrine, and rectitude in life. Of these things not even the Devil himself will be able to rob a man, if he who possesses them guards them with the needful carefulness.

NONE CAN HARM HIM WHO DOES NOT INJURE HIMSELF

A carpenter makes a box. First he has the box in design; for if he had it not in design, how could he produce it by workmanship? But the box in theory is not the very box as it appears to the eyes. It exists invisibly in design, it will be visible in the work. Behold, it is made in the work; has it ceased to exist in design? The one is made in the work, and the other remains which exists in design; for that box may rot, and another be fashioned according to that which exists in design. Give heed, then, to the box as it is in design, and the box as it is in fact. The actual box is not life, the box in design is life; because the soul of the artificer, where all these things are before they are brought forth, is living. So, dearly beloved brethren, because the Wisdom of God, by which all things have been made, contains everything according to design before it is made, therefore those things which are made through this design itself are not forthwith life, but whatever has been made is life in him. You see the earth, there is an earth in design; you see the sky, there is a sky in design; you see the sun and the moon, these also exist in design; but externally they are bodies, in design they are life.

HOMILIES ON SAINT MATTHEW

LET us also imitate him, and despair of no one. For the fishermen, too, when they have cast many times have not succeeded; but afterwards having cast again, have gained all. So we also expect that ye will all at once show to us ripe fruit. For the husbandman, too, after he has sown, waits one day or two days, and is a long while in expectation; and all at once he sees the fruits springing up on every side.

HOMILIES ON SAINT MATTHEW

As many as stand indebted to thee, either for money or for trespasses, let them all go free, and require of God the recompense of such thy magnanimity. For so long as they continue indebted to thee, thou canst not have God thy debtor. But if thou let them go free, thou wilt be able to detain thy God, and to require of him the recompense of so great self-restraint in bountiful measure. For suppose a man had come up and seeing thee arresting thy debtor, had called upon thee to let him go free, and transfer to himself thy account with the other; he would not choose to be unfair after such remission, seeing he had passed the whole demand to himself; how then shall God fail to repay us manifold, yea, ten thousandfold, when for his commandment's sake, if any be indebted to us, we urge no complaint against them, great or small, but let them go exempt from all liability? Let us not then think of the temporary pleasure that springs up in us by exacting of our debtors, but of the loss, rather, how great! which we shall thereby sustain hereafter, grievously injuring ourselves in the things which are eternal. Rising accordingly above all, let us forgive those who must give account to us, both their debts and their offenses; that we may make our own accounts prove indulgent, and that what we could not reach by all virtue besides, this we may obtain by not bearing malice against our neighbors; and thus enjoy the eternal blessings, by the grace and love toward man of our Lord Jesus Christ, to whom be glory and might now and always, even forever and ever.

HOMILIES ON SAINT MATTHEW

SHOULDEST thou run into grief, take heed lest the tyranny of despondency pervert thy tongue, but that thou speak like Christ. For he too mourned for Lazarus and Judas. Shouldest thou fall into fear, seek again to speak even as he. For he himself fell into fear for thy sake, with regard to his manhood. Do thou also say, "Nevertheless, not as I will, but as thou wilt."

And if thou shouldest lament, weep calmly as he. Shouldest thou fall into plots and sorrows, treat these, too, as Christ. For indeed he had plots laid against him, and was in sorrow, and saith, "My soul is exceeding sorrowful, even unto death." And all the examples he presented to thee, in order that thou shouldest continually observe the same measures, and not destroy the rules that have been given thee. So shalt thou be able to have a mouth like his mouth, so while treading on the earth, thou wilt show forth a tongue like to that of him who sits on high; thou wilt maintain the limits he observed in despondency, in anger, in suffering, in agony.

How many are they of you that desire to see his form? Behold, it is possible, not to see him only, but also to become like him; if we are in earnest.

HOMILIES ON SAINT JOHN

IF any man hath thorns, let him cast the fire of the Spirit amongst them. If any hath a hard and stubborn heart, let him by employing the same fire make it soft and yielding. If any by the wayside is trodden down by all kind of thoughts, let him enter into more sheltered places, and not lie exposed for those that will to invade for plunder: that so we may see your cornfields waving with corn. Besides, if we exercise such care as this over ourselves, and apply

ourselves industriously to this spiritual hearing, if not only
once yet by degrees, we shall surely be free from all the
cares of life.

HOMILIES ON SAINT MATTHEW

LET us all humble our own souls by almsgiving and
forgiving our neighbors their trespasses, by not
remembering injuries, nor avenging ourselves. If we
continually reflect on our sins, no external circumstances
can make us elated: neither riches, nor power, nor
authority, nor honor; nay, even should we sit in the
imperial chariot itself, we shall sigh bitterly: Since even the
blessed David was a king, and yet he said, "Every night I
will wash my bed," and he was not at all hurt by the
purple robe and the diadem; he was not puffed up; for he
knew himself to be a man, and inasmuch as his heart had
been made contrite, he went mourning.

For what are all things human? Ashes and dust, and as
it were spray before the wind; a smoke and a shadow, and
a leaf driven here and there; and a flower; a dream, and a
tale, and a fable, wind and air vainly puffed out and
wasting away; a feather that hath no stay, a stream flowing
by, or if there be aught of more nothingness than these.

For, tell me, what dost thou esteem great? What
dignity thinkest thou to be great? Is it that of the consul?
For the many think no greater dignity than that. He who is
not consul is not a whit inferior to him who is in so great
splendor, who is so greatly admired. Both one and the
other are of the same dignity; both of them alike, after a
little while, are no more.

HOMILIES ON HEBREWS

VII. Mystical Wisdom

Thou that instructeth Christians in thy heavenly wisdom!
Guide us to that topmost height of mystic lore
which exceedeth light and more than exceedeth
knowledge.

DIONYSIUS

WE close with a mediation attributed to Dionysius the Areopagite, but actually written about the turn of the sixth century by a Syrian churchman, who was a neo-Platonic theologian and mystic. *The Mystical Theology* is a celebration of the mystery of God. Instead of projecting God's nature from a survey of God's attributes, the author uses these same qualities to define what God is not. This method, familiar to mystics ever since, is called the *via negativa*: because God is ineffable, God cannot be described in words, and every description of God, however exalted, therefore limits our appreciation of God's true nature. In this rapturous meditation, Pseudo-Dionysius invites us to transcend the rational realm and enter the realm of pure spirit and power in order to approach a more perfect mystical union with the Divine.

Here, meditation begins to take on a new meaning, one familiar in Oriental religious traditions but also characteristic of mystics of every faith and time. As Pseudo-Dionysius puts it, when we meditate in our quest for mystical union, we recognize that our goal is not achievable by "any act of reason or understanding; nor can it be described by the reason or perceived by the understanding . . . nor can the reason attain to it to name it or to know it. . . . It transcends all affirmation by being the perfect and unique cause of all things, and transcends all negation by the preeminence of its simple and absolute nature—free from every limitation and beyond them all."

The tension between the Greek inclination toward meditation as a form of union with God and the Latin tendency to regard it as an ethical inspiration is transcended for at least a moment of profound reverie. Dionysius invites us to participate in a God unapproachably beyond us who at the same time is the wellspring of our inner being.

THIRTEEN

The Meditations of Dionysius

I

TRINITY, which exceedeth all Being, Deity, and Goodness! Thou that instructeth Christians in thy heavenly wisdom! Guide us to that topmost height of mystic lore which exceedeth light and more than exceedeth knowledge, where the simple, absolute, and unchangeable mysteries of heavenly Truth lie hidden in the dazzling obscurity of the secret Silence, outshining all brilliance with the intensity of their darkness, and surcharging our blinded intellects with the utterly impalpable and invisible fairness of glories which exceed all beauty! Such be my prayer; . . . I counsel that, in the earnest exercise of mystic contemplation, thou leave the senses and the activities of the intellect and all things that the senses or the intellect can perceive, and all things in this world of nothingness, or in that world of being, and that, thine understanding being laid to rest, thou strain (so far as thou mayest) toward a union with him whom neither being nor understanding can contain. For, by the unceasing and absolute renunciation of thyself and all things, thou shalt in pureness cast all things aside, and be released from all, and so shalt be led upwards to the ray of that divine Darkness which exceedeth all existence.

These things thou must not disclose to any of the uninitiated, by whom I mean those who cling to the objects of human thought, and imagine there is no super-essential reality beyond, and fancy that they know by human understanding him that has made Darkness his secret place. And if the Divine Initiation is beyond such men as these, what can be said of others yet more incapable thereof, who describe the Transcendent Cause of all things by qualities drawn from the lowest order of being, while they deny that it is in any way superior to the various ungodly delusions which they fondly invent in ignorance of this truth? That while it possesses all the positive attributes of the universe (being the universal Cause), yet in a stricter sense it does not posses them, since it transcends them all, wherefore there is no contradiction between affirming and denying that it has them inasmuch as it precedes and surpasses all deprivation, being beyond all positive and negative distinctions?

Such at least is the teaching of the blessed Bartholomew. For he says that the subject matter of the Divine Science is vast and yet minute, and that the Gospel combines in itself both width and straitness. Methinks he has shown by these his words how marvelously he has understood that the Good Cause of all things is eloquent yet speaks few words, or rather none; possessing neither speech nor understanding because it exceedeth all things in a super-essential manner, and is revealed in its naked truth to those alone who pass right through the opposition of fair and foul, and pass beyond the topmost altitudes of the holy ascent and leave behind them all divine enlightenment and voices and heavenly utterances and plunge into the Darkness where truly dwells, as saith the Scripture, that One which is beyond all things. For not without reason is the blessed Moses bidden first to undergo purification himself and then to separate himself from those who have not undergone it; and after all purification hears the many-voiced trumpets and sees many lights flash forth with pure and diverse-streaming rays, and then stands separate from the multitudes and with the chosen priests presses forward to the topmost pinnacle of the Divine Ascent. Nevertheless he meets not with God himself, yet he beholds—not him indeed (for he is invisible)—but the place wherein he dwells. And this I take to signify that the divinest and the highest of the things perceived by the eyes of the body or the mind are but the symbolic language of things subordinate to him who himself transcendeth them all. Through these things his incomprehensible presence is shown walking upon those heights of his holy places which are perceived by the mind; and then it breaks forth, even from the things that are beheld and from those that behold them, and plunges the true initiate unto the Darkness of Unknowing wherein he renounces all the apprehensions of his understanding and is enwrapped in that which is wholly intangible and invisible, belonging wholly to him that is beyond all things and to none else (whether himself or another), and being through the passive stillness of all his reasoning powers united by his highest faculty to him that is wholly Unknowable, of whom thus by a rejection of all knowledge he possesses a knowledge that exceeds his understanding.

II

Unto this Darkness which is beyond Light we pray that we may come, and may attain unto vision through the loss of sight and knowledge, and that in ceasing thus to see or to know we may learn to know that which is beyond all perception and understanding (for this emptying of our faculties is true sight and knowledge), and that we may offer him that transcends all things the praises of a transcendent hymnody, which we shall do by denying or removing all things that are—like as men who, carving a statue out of marble, remove all the impediments that hinder the clear perceptive of the latent image and by this mere removal display the hidden statue itself in its hidden beauty. Now we must wholly distinguish this negative method from that of positive statements. For when we were making positive statements we began with the most universal statements, and then through intermediate terms we came at last to particular titles, but now ascending upward from particular to universal conceptions we strip off all qualities in order that we may attain a naked knowledge of that Unknowing which in all existent things is enwrapped by all objects of knowledge, and that we may begin to see that super-essential Darkness which is hidden by all the light that is in existent things.

III

The universal Cause transcending all things is neither impersonal nor lifeless, nor irrational nor without understanding; in short, that It is not a material body, and therefore does not possess outward shape or intelligible form or quality or quantity or solid weight; nor has it any local existence which can be perceived by sight or touch; nor has it the power of perceiving or being perceived; nor does it suffer any vexation or disorder through the disturbance of earthly passions, or any feebleness through the tyranny of material chances, or any want of light; nor any change, or decay, or division, or deprivation, or ebb and flow, or anything else which the senses can perceive. None of these things can be either identified with it or attributed unto it.

IV

Once more, ascending yet higher we maintain that It is not soul, or mind, or endowed with the faculty of imagination, conjecture, reason, or understanding; nor is it any act of reason or understanding; nor can it be described by the reason or perceived by the understanding, since it is not number or order or greatness or littleness or equality or inequality, and since it is not immovable nor in motion, or at rest, and has no power, and is not power or light, and does not live, and is not life; nor is it personal essence, or eternity, or time; nor can it be grasped by the understanding, since it is not knowledge or truth; nor is it kingship or wisdom; nor is it one, nor is it unity, nor is it Godhead or Goodness; nor is it a Spirit, as we understand the term, since it is not Sonship or Fatherhood; nor is it any other thing such as we or any other being can have knowledge of; nor does it belong to the category of nonexistence or to that of existence; nor do existent beings know it as it actually is, nor does it know them as they actually are; nor can the reason attain to it to name it or to know it; nor is it darkness, nor is it light, or error, or truth; nor can any affirmation or negation apply to it; for while applying affirmations or negations to those orders of being that come next to it, we apply not unto it either affirmation or negation, inasmuch as it transcends all affirmation by being the perfect and unique Cause of all things, and transcends all negation by the preeminence of its simple and absolute nature—free from every limitation and beyond them all.

S O U R C E   A N D   N A M E   I N D E X

DEVOTION AND TOPICAL INDEX

F. FORRESTER CHURCH is Senior Minister of All Souls Unitarian Church in New York City. He is editor of Macmillan's *The Essential Tillich* and author of *Father & Son, The Devil & Dr. Church, Entertaining Angels, The Seven Deadly Virtues, Everyday Miracles,* and *Our Chosen Faith: An Introduction to Unitarian Universalism* (with John Buehrens). Dr. Church received his Ph.D. in 1978 from Harvard University in the field of Early Church History.

TERRENCE J. MULRY received his B.A. in Religion and master's degree in International Affairs from Columbia University, after which he worked for ten years in publishing. He is co-editor (with Dr. Church) of *The Macmillan Book of Earliest Christian Prayers* and *The Macmillan Book of Earliest Christian Hymns.* Mr. Mulry is in his third year of the Master of Divinity program at Harvard Divinity School.